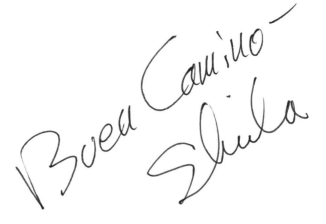

Found Along The Way

STORIES FROM THE
CAMINO DE SANTIAGO

SHEILA KOGAN

D1474907

Found Along The Way

STORIES FROM THE CAMINO DE SANTIAGO

SHEILA KOGAN

Published by Sand Hill Review Press
www.sandhillreviewpress.com,
1 Baldwin Ave, #304, San Mateo, CA 94401

ISBN: 978-1-949534-22-1 Perfect bound
ISBN: 978-1-949534-23-8 epub
Library of Congress Control Number: 2020924711

Cataloging-in-Publication data:
Names: Kogan, Sheila, author.
Title: Found along the way : stories from the Camino de
Santiago / Sheila Kogan.
Description: San Mateo, CA: Sand Hill Review Press, 2021.
Identifiers: LCCN: 2020924711 | ISBN: 978-1-949534-22-1
(paperback) | 978-1-949534-23-8 (ebook)
Subjects: LCSH Kogan, Sheila--Travel--Camino de Santiago
de Compostela.| Camino de Santiago de Compostela. |
Spain--Description and travel. | Aging. | Self-actualization
(Psychology) | Spiritual biography. | BISAC BIOGRAPHY &
AUTOBIOGRAPHY / Personal Memoirs
Classification: LCC BX2321.S3 K64 2021 | DDC 914.6/11--dc23

Art Direction by Tory Hartmann, Sand Hill Review Press
Graphics by Backspace Ink.

SHRP
Sand Hill Review Press
1 BALDWIN AVE, #304, SAN MATEO, CA 94401

Introductory Note

WHEN I CAME BACK from walking the Camino de Santiago in 2011, people asked how it was and, even though I was in my late sixties, I stammered like a teenager. "Like totally amazing!" I couldn't talk about it. There was no way to pull apart the rich multilayered sensations of the trip—but I found I could tell stories. I was able to recount the time I picked up a sandal or got a massage or met Meg or got lost. So here they are, a loose sequence of twenty perspectives from my journey across Spain and deep into myself.

The stories all happened. They are true *as far as memory holds*. I understand how slippery it is to remember; time changes what stands out and how it fits together. When I picked up the sandal it created an interesting event, later I became more aware of my internal conflict dealing with it, and only much later did I consider what would have happened if I had walked by. Having worked on these stories for eight years, they come with layers of memory. Of course I consulted my journal, photographs, and, when possible, someone who was there. My main objective, however, has been to capture the truth of each experience as I felt it.

Because the stories tell about different aspects of the journey, they do not march straight forward in time and place. They go forward and backward, and sometimes encounters are mentioned more than once as they are seen from different angles. You will meet Richard and Gandhi and visit Astorga a few times. A map of the route is included.

Five of the stories are Extraordinary Encounters. These are—dare I call them?—visions or conversations with God. I know that sounds presumptuous and I can imagine eyes rolled back and books slammed shut. I get it; it's a bit much. Yet they happened and are the experiences for which I am the most grateful. I want to share their resonance as I tell them here for the first time.

But on to practical notes: The words *hostel, refuge, shelter,* and *albergue* are used interchangeably and refer to sleeping arrangements where you rent a bed for the night. The bed might be in a large dormitory or clustered into smaller rooms but everything is communal and public; bathrooms are gender designated or mixed. *Pensions* and *B&B's* provide individual rooms with shared bathrooms. This is not a handbook and I offer few tips; I refer you to my invaluable, now completely dog-eared and I-will-never-throw-it-away guide: *A Pilgrim's Guide to the Camino de Santiago: St. Jean, Roncesvalles, Santiago* by John Brierley

Hospitalero/a is the person who manages an *albergue*. *Peregrino* means pilgrim and that is about all the Spanish I know.

Most names have been changed.

There are times I find it hard to believe I went on this trip. I'm doubtful I could physically manage it now. The encounters and events were, well, totally amazing—in retrospect they seem unbelievable. That is when I pull out the picture of Thomas or grasp the lovely stone given to me by a Buddhist nun, and find myself right back on the trail. I am grateful to have walked this pilgrimage and just as thankful to relive it through writing. Come on the journey with me and see.

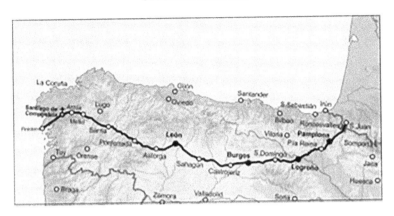

I started at Roncesvalles and walked to Santiago, 780 kilometers, which translates to 484.67 miles, not counting explorations and wrong turns. Finisterre is 89 kilometers, 55.3 miles, farther than Santiago on the very point of the continent.

Acknowledgements

Right before I left, my late sister-in-law, who thought I was crazy, said, "If you are ever in trouble, I will be there in a day." I am grateful to all my family and friends who supported this trip despite their trepidations. I thank Barbara Hawkins for her brilliant and bold editing, Jennifer Bentley and Gail Alter for their consistent help. Many thanks to all my advance readers, especially Patsy Paul, Sr. Kathleen McCabe, and Suelene Lee, for their invaluable notes. I would be up a creek without Olivia Benowitz. And I always bow to Alon Shalev and the Berkeley Writers Group for keeping me on track.

I am most grateful to God for walking with me.

Dedication

To Reed, who I believe is in a happier place.
To all pilgrims: Buen Camino.

Contents

15

Prologue: Pulling the Thread

STEPPING ONTO THE PATIO in back of the hostel, I saw an assortment of pilgrims sitting around a rough-hewn table littered with beer and wine bottles. The light was just beginning to fade and an evening breeze swayed the large-leafed trees enclosing the courtyard. Bright red geraniums bobbed their heads. The small gathering waved and called out.

"Another one. Welcome."

"Come join us."

I had been walking for almost two weeks and was used to joining pilgrims at the end of the day. But now I had just said goodbye to a Camino friend who was continuing on, and I did not feel like chatting. Hesitantly, I approached the raucous group—and soon found myself drawn in.

As it usually happened, the conversation turned to the most frequent Camino question: Why had we come?

Nigel, a tall middle-aged British professor, responded first. In a voice that sounded like BBC news he said, "Well Nat and I are off on a bloody adventure. It's her twenty-fifth birthday." As we cheered and toasted her, he dabbed his lips with a napkin then draped his arm around Natalie's shoulders. Natalie, his young Italian travel companion, did

17

not look up but held her wine glass in two hands and slurped as if it were soup.

"Yah, I go on the adventure," announced Magda. Swedish, probably in her mid-forties, she had a muscular body and an open, no-nonsense face. She continued, "I change job so take a month away before start. Leave my husband with four children." Her gleeful laughter infused the entire group with abandon.

Hans Jakob, a prim Austrian man, said, "I have just retired after forty years as headmaster of a secondary school and I am looking for a challenge. I want to see if I can do it." We all nodded agreement, clamoring to tell about our physical trials on the Camino. The conversation whirled about and then wound down. Almost breathless we sat back and watched the evening deepen.

Directing his gaze at me, Hans Jakob asked, "Eh, San Francisco, what brought you here?"

I produced my generic reply: "I'm not crazy about the idea of getting old and, well, wanted to do something different."

It was true—partially. At sixty-six I felt poised to either pull up a rocking chair or do something astounding, and tramping across Spain by myself seemed extreme enough. Of course there was more, and that night, curled in my sleeping bag, I mulled over my motives. Why had a non-hiking, anti-backpacking, limited-Spanish-speaking, saint-resisting Jewish-Catholic skeptic chosen to follow the Way of Saint James?

Pulling that thread seemed to unravel the entire sweater of my life.

* * * *

AS A YOUNG CHILD I decided the universe was dangerous.

When I was three years old my family fled from Egypt and I vividly recalled the threatening, hate-filled eyes of the Egyptian border guards rifling through our belongings. As we settled in the United States, I found not so much hatred as derision: My Midwestern classmates giggled at my embroidered smock, my accent, my incomprehension of the game *Duck Duck Goose.* Later as a university student in Berkeley, I encountered the violence of police indiscriminately spraying and clubbing observers during the Vietnam War protests—their batons left dark bruises on my back and arms and psyche.

Experience pointed to a world full of malice and menace. Not surprisingly I grew up somewhat timid: I feared heights, speed, horror movies, and the dark. More, I was convinced that outcomes were up to me and skeptical that things actually worked out for the best.

Yet ... Something else brewed within me, an opposite universe with a completely different outlook. Alongside my cynical worldview, I experienced the joy and calm of a loving divinity. Like a tug toward faith—what else would I call that quiet relentless pull?—I felt drawn to a path and a Presence. I had to consider the possibility that there was a God and that He was with me.

I remember my first encounter with the divine. It was one afternoon when I was about eight years old. Having been in the States for a few years, I had accustomed myself to a sense of isolation, but that day I was feeling especially alone as I walked my dog in the field across the street from my house. Watching the golden sunset I suddenly sensed a glowing warmth. I felt embraced by peace and unity and love. The extravagance of sensation totally transformed the chilly day and I went home awed and thrilled—but never spoke a word about it.

I treasured that experience and tucked it away with other inexplicable events, like the time I skidded across multiple lanes of traffic and stepped out of a wrecked car without a scratch. These occurrences made no sense in the everyday world—unless I included a caring God. I walked the path of a skeptic while a parallel stream gurgled nearby. Sometimes I heard it, often I did not. The divine tug led me on a circuitous spiritual quest, rambling through Transcendental Meditation, Buddhism, and the Gurdjieff mysteries, until I found my spiritual home in the Catholic Church.

Now I was sitting at a table with a boisterous group of pilgrims. I couldn't reveal that I thought God had led me to this pilgrimage; I'd sound like a wild-eyed religious fanatic. And, if truth be told, I was struggling to accept that conjecture myself. Nor did I want to expose the intimate details of how the beginning of the Camino had started six years earlier, the day I numbly sat on the edge of my bed feeling like I had lost a vital organ.

* * * *

I HAD JUST FLOWN IN from Okinawa via Tokyo, through exhausting date and time changes, taken the subway and a cab home, walked in the door, put my suitcase down, and picked up the phone.

Reaching my lawyer, I got straight to the point, "Let's finalize that divorce."

It had taken my husband three months to convince me to join him in Okinawa. The plan was to visit our son who was stationed there and put our thirty-year marriage back on track. After a couple of days with him I found he had simultaneously wooed a Thai woman our son's age and established a residence with her in Thailand. Kissing my son goodbye, I immediately headed to the airport.

Coming home after that long flight, I sat immobile on the bed feeling at the very edge of my life. Having worked throughout the marriage, I did not feel helpless so much as lost. Grief and anger lay dormant under the barrage of immediate details. How would I get the taxes done, or start the lawn mower, or fix the computer? And would I ever travel again? I was sixty-one and couldn't imagine going anywhere alone.

I got up from the bed and walked to the kitchen to start a list. Tomorrow I would have to find a tax preparer and handyman, then search the local newspaper for someone to look at that big, old desktop computer that kept freezing up.

* * * *

HE CAME TO FIX my computer and I thought maybe this could be a new man in my life. The credentials were right: tall, athletic, the right age, practically a neighbor, and a jazz musician as well as a computer nerd. I noticed his body looked stiff, like a puppet bending only at the joints, and his voice sounded strained, as if his collar was buttoned too tight. *Don't be so picky,* I scolded myself.

"That should do it," Reed said patting the machine. He seemed quite surprised that he was able to fix my computer.

He's got my contact info. I bet he calls to ask me out.

Sure enough, after the appropriate three days, he asked me out to dinner.

"I'd be delighted."

Choosing what I recalled after three decades was standard first-date attire, I put on a black skirt and pale blue sweater-set and waited. And waited. After almost an hour I gave up and called and—woke him up.

"Oh, oh, okay, I'll meet you there," he fumbled.

"What? You want to meet me at the restaurant?" Even in my own ears it sounded like a screech.

"Oh, oh, I'll pick you up."

That is how Reed and I started our confused friendship. He was a new man in my life but absolutely not the romance I had in mind. I assigned him a peripheral friend role: meals, jazz, and walks. Both of us wanted more but our dating introduction left each of us out of sync with the other. Isn't it said that timing trumps everything?

But we both loved to walk and it was on these long ambles that Reed introduced me to the Camino. I had never heard of it. I didn't know that Santiago was the Spanish combination of Saint and Iago (James), knew nothing about venerated buried bones, the field of light, or a hiking trail drawing pilgrims for over a thousand years. Popes and peasants and St. Francis had walked it; Paul Coelho, Shirley MacLaine, and countless others had written about it.

Reed had walked the Camino five and a half times—the half being when he blew out his knee and had to stop—and he asserted repeatedly, "It's the happiest I have been in my whole life."

Strapping on a heavy backpack, trudging fifteen or twenty miles, then sleeping in a hostel hemmed in by snoring pilgrims was my image of hell. "Sounds awful," I declared.

But I had not realized how Reed's love of the trail had sown a seed. Unobserved it took root as the intriguing idea of walking without turning around and it became a pull to just consider going. Other factors, like my volunteer work in a homeless center (Chapter 2), also converged to draw me toward the pilgrimage. The desire to walk the Camino seemed to have a will of its own. Like a boulder coming loose from a cliffside, the ground had been softened by a number of influences but the pull was gravitational.

I bought my first pair of hiking boots and began training with tuna cans in my pack. My son gave me a set of walking poles and I reluctantly learned how to wield them. Reed planned to come with me and it occurred to me that we might look at each other differently on foreign ground, but he hesitated buying a plane ticket, said he was not feeling too well.

* * * *

"THAT RAIN JACKET is too heavy," Reed said, looking over the gear spread out on my living room couch. "You need a thin one to go over your layering system. And get rain pants too."

"I'm going to need rain pants?" My experience of walking in the rain consisted of dashing to the car. "And what the hell is a *layering system*? The weather's going to be that extreme?" Walking across Spain suddenly felt overwhelming, too unknown, too scary. I could not possibly do it by myself. "You have to come with me. I can't do it. Why won't you go?" My voice had climbed in pitch and volume.

Reed gazed past me. He looked so sad something within me shifted, like a combination lock clicking one notch to open. I realized I had been focused completely on myself—my trip, my gear, my fear. My voice softened to a murmur, "Why aren't you going?"

He waited a while before answering, absentmindedly fingering my folded wicking shirt. I let the silence linger.

"I've scheduled an experimental surgery for my stomach cancer."

I held in a gasp and just stared at him. I wanted to scream: Why didn't you tell me? How bad is it? Are you in pain? Instead I whispered, "All these years ... I never knew."

"No, no one knew but my brother. I don't want to see the pity in people's eyes."

I checked if I was projecting pity but could not fathom what my face showed in the jumble of emotions. I just blinked.

"I have something for you," Reed said, as he pulled his backpack closer. No matter where he went, Reed always carried a small pack and wore a hiking hat. He pulled out two champagne corks with holes in the middle.

"These are for your walking poles," he said with a childlike grin. "I made them for you." Reaching in the pack again he pulled out a fairly large, white clamshell with a small hole drilled through the top. "And hang this from your pack. It's the symbol of a pilgrim."

"Gosh," was the only word I could articulate. I felt the weight of Reed sharing his deepest love with me.

Cradling my strange treasures, I was taken aback by the turn of events, how things so often were not as they appeared. *Perception is not always reality*, I reminded myself.

But something else was swirling into my consciousness: our initial date. I started wondering about Reed being asleep when we were supposed to meet that first time. Maybe it had not been ineptitude or carelessness. Maybe he was asleep because he was sick. I did not want to think about the possibility of lost chances.

"Go walk the Camino," Reed said. "You can do it."

1—The Ticket

"WHAT IF I DIE out there?" I turned to my son for reassurance. "Just joking ... sort of."

"Hell of a way to go, Mom."

Grinning, he pulled up to the airline terminal, jumped out and swung my backpack out of the trunk. "Safe travels," he whispered, giving me a quick, tight hug. Then he added, "By the way, happy Mother's Day."

I bared my teeth into what I hoped would pass for a smile and waved goodbye. He slid back into the driver's seat, honked twice, and vanished into the rush of vehicles.

Standing outside San Francisco International I stared after the car long after it had disappeared. My stomach lurched in my high-tech microfiber hiking pants. Did I have to pee again? I was three months shy of my sixty-seventh birthday, had traveled alone only once, and had not quite finished lesson three in my Spanish speaking CDs. What was I thinking heading off to walk across Spain—the width of a whole country—by myself?

Still staring after the long-gone car, I thought how different this Mother's Day was from last year. A year ago my own mother was still alive. My sons had taken me to a champagne brunch at a restaurant with pink tablecloths and three-fork place settings and then we had gone to my mother's nursing home to celebrate the holiday with her. I had worn sandaled heels with red, manicured toenails peeking out. Now my painted toes were encased in grey boat-sized hiking boots and breakfast consisted of a granola bar eaten on the way to the airport.

My backpack leaned cockily against the curb, daring me to go. Despite people swirling around me, I felt completely alone—as disconnected as a speck of dust suspended in sunlight. My chest flip-flopped in its wacked-out way and for the hundredth time I patted the top pouch to make sure my heart medication was nearby. Hoisting the pack over one shoulder, I tightened my grip on the e-ticket printout and approached the massive revolving door.

After checking in I headed uneasily to security. My medium-size pack had collapsible walking poles strapped to the sides and I worried the security guards might see them as weapons. Before leaving I had replaced Reed's hand-made champagne cork tips for standard rubber shields. The new tips were more useful but I missed having a part of my friend with me in his crazy corks. The clamshell he had given me dangled from the back zipper, identifying me as a pilgrim. Hoping that chutzpa would get me through, I left the poles where they were and tried to look nonchalant. The agent smiled leniently and waved me on as if I were a child pretending to be Superman.

I boarded the plane clutching my pack to my chest like a security blanket, stored it overhead, and sank into my seat. As the plane began its rattling takeoff, my head began its relentless buzz. How presumptuous of me to attempt this pilgrimage and even more arrogant to imagine that the Creator of the Universe had stooped to beckon a speck of dust. Why would He?

Yet ... Was that the barest brush of hope whispering to me? *Just ahead.*

Blowing up my inflatable neck-rest, I pushed the seat back and closed my eyes. My mind went all the way back to my first glimpse of the divine when, as a child, I was awed seeing grace in a sunset. I went on to pursue several religious paths early in my life, but at close to forty was still seeking a spiritual home when a friend gave me a Bible that divided the Old and New Testaments into daily readings. Giving her cursory thanks I threw it in the back of my car with the unused yoga mat. I remember thinking, *I don't have the time to read the Bible everyday. What kind of fanatic does that?*

I knew my hesitancy was much deeper. As a Jew I grew up with the message that it was not permissible to read the New Testament and certainly not allowed to utter Christ's name. What led me, then, a year after it was given to me, to pull that book out, dust it off, and quietly read it? Over and over. Every day. For ten years.

The flight attendant stopped the snack cart alongside me. I wasn't sure if I was hungry or my stomach was churning with nerves.

"Just water, thanks," I said. For a seven-week trip I needed to parcel money carefully. I would wait and eat on the international flight.

Closing my eyes again I pictured that Bible, which still sat next to my bed. I found it hard to believe that I used to get up before my pre-school children awoke. Every morning I would stagger into the living room shaking off the ache to stay in bed, then turn on one light and curl up in my armchair with a cup of tea. In the pre-dawn darkness I read a daily section, encountering unimagined possibilities of who Christ was. The more times I reread Scriptures the more it seemed that the Old and New Testaments were one story; but if I acknowledged that, the path pointed to the Incarnation ... and the Messiah.

After a decade of study, the pages were worn soft and I was worn down from grappling with ideas forbidden to me. I had started reading the Bible when my children were toddlers and now they were young teens. It was enough, I decided. Time to put up or shut the book.

* * * *

"I DON'T WANT to convert. I just have some questions," I told the adult conversion class as I tapped my three-ring binder.

Father Seamus asked, "How many questions do you have?" His Irish lilt included a dash of whimsy.

"Three hundred and sixteen."

His eyes crinkled as he looked at me steadily then sighed. "Well, we'd better get at it. What's the first one?"

"Why did Jesus say, 'My God, my God, why have you abandoned me?'"

Eight months later I stood in front of the congregation. I could pick out my husband and sons smiling at me; they found my new direction strange but respected my lengthy deliberations. Father Seamus arced over me with a pitcher and sprinkled holy water on my forehead, careful not to muss my hair too much. I felt the drops land; they stung as if they were acid. Turning away from his microphone he whispered, "That wasn't so bad was it?"

Thinking about the ten-year struggle that led up to this moment and a presentiment of what lay ahead, I whispered back, "Yes, it was."

* * * *

I NEVER INTENDED to tell my mother about my conversion but one day at lunch she cornered me. It was one of my twice-yearly visits and we were eating salads on the veranda of a fashionable restaurant near her house. Huge ceramic pots holding palms and pink impatiens circled around us like gossipy neighbors.

Referring to my youngest son, she said, "It's about time you enrolled him in Hebrew school." I had heard that reproach countless times with my other two boys and it made me slump with weariness.

My mind drifted and I imagined sipping a chilled glass of chardonnay. My mother disapproved of alcohol and would have been horrified if I ordered wine with lunch. But it was so enticing I toyed with the idea, dreamily considering whether I would prefer a sauvignon blanc. I was fed up hedging about my sons, hiding my faith, distorting my life for her.

"Mom," I started hesitantly, my voice sounded far away, as if it came from someone else. "I have been on a ... kind of a ... faith journey. I have been reading the Bible and ..."

"So you joined the temple?" She smiled hopefully. My family attended synagogue for holidays though we never spoke of faith or God.

"No, Mom, actually I believe ... uh ... I have come to believe ..." Sweat rolled down the back of my neck and the side of my face as my senses heightened into every crevice of the moment: I was aware of the hard edge of the chair against my butt, the greens and yellows of the salad, the crackling of ice melting in my water glass.

I looked directly into my mother's glaring eyes. "I believe Jesus was the Messiah," I blurted.

"What?" she screeched, managing to contain the sound so we did not cause a scene.

"I believe Jesus—"

"What? Who got to you? Who warped your mind?" Her eyes narrowed.

"No one. This is something I've been studying for a long time and— "

"Somebody had to poison you," she said. Her face twisted into a sneer and referring to the man I chose to call Lord, she spit out, "He was a bastard you know."

She had pierced me. My body flamed in anger and shame and horror. The slippery avocado stuck in my throat.

The waitress bustled over. "How are we doing here?" she asked in high-pitched cheeriness. "Can I show you the dessert menu?"

I shook my head no and whispered hoarsely, "Check, please."

My mother's face appeared frozen as she leaned forward. "You are dead to me."

People talked and ate and the palm leaves rustled around us.

Two days later my sister called.

"I'm calling for Mom," she began with no hello.

"Oh?" A faint glimmer of hope that my mother would accept me squeaked through the sentries guarding my heart.

"She wants to know if you could just become a Buddhist."

The wish evaporated. Despite the disappointment, my body shook in silent laughter. My mother must have heard about Bujews.

"No, I'm Catholic," I answered.

"Then you're ruined?"

It sounded like my sister was asking if I was a deflowered virgin. "What do you mean?"

"Are you ..." She inhaled sharply. "Are you ... baptized?"

"Yes."

"There's nothing to say."

My family did not talk to me for five years.

No big deal, I tried to convince myself. *The separation doesn't really affect me. Kids, husband, work are all the same,* I reiterated with regularity. But I had swallowed their scorn and it sat in the pit of my stomach like a stone.

* * * *

MY BODY RECOILED with the memory. The sound of jet engines filled my ears as I twisted my Holy Mother medallion. The neck-rest had lost all its air and I discarded it under the seat. I got up and wandered to the back of the plane.

Two flights, one subway ride, one bus ride, and a twenty-minute walk past the mammoth grey-stone sites of downtown Madrid—twenty-two hours with no sleep and little food—I stood at the door of my modest hotel. Blue paint was peeling around the beveled glass of what once had been an elegant building.

Drained and disconnected yet excited about being in Spain for the first time, I smiled bravely as I approached the mild looking desk clerk.

"*Buenos dias.*" Even to my own ears I sounded like a country hick.

"Welcome, *Señora.*" He nodded with a little bow.

I signed in and climbed the narrow creaking stairs. My tiny hotel room had faded pink rose wallpaper, lace curtains, and a flowered quilt. Shrugging the pack off, I rubbed my sore shoulders. I had only walked one mile and my back was groaning. Carrying nineteen pounds through the streets of Madrid renewed my drive to weed out what was unnecessary.

Dumping my pack on the floral bedcover, I scrutinized the contents for excess. First to go was the romance novel I brought for the plane—I tore out the chapters I had finished and ripped off the back cover—then I cut my clothesline in half, threw away all the clothespins but four, and shed the extra tube of body lotion. That eliminated two ounces. At this point I thought the ounce of eye makeup was still a necessity. There was nothing else to discard.

I repacked, neatly layering my sleeping bag and mat, sandals (each primly encased in a plastic bag) and a stuff sack containing a few clothes. Toiletries and raingear were stowed in outer pouches. That was it. There were no spares and no choices about what to wear. I was stripped bare.

Sitting on the bed, I put my head in my hands. *Are You there, Lord? If You don't walk with me I am bare-assed naked out here. Don't abandon me.*

The little bed in the third-floor room in the middle of Madrid squeaked as I stretched out remembering the time my family had abandoned me. And how abruptly I was pulled back into the fold.

* * * *

THE FIVE YEARS of silence ended when my mother started forgetting to turn off the burners of her stove. After a fire brigade had to put out a blaze, my siblings called.

"Hello?" Even after all that time I immediately recognized my sister's voice.

"We have a place for Mom in the Jewish Home in San Francisco," my sister said. "Can you move her?"

The request made sense since I was a six-hour drive from our mother while my siblings lived across the country. But it was as if nothing had happened. The estrangement had been erased. All reactions and recriminations were packed, sealed, and stowed away in a paid storage unit—the cost being a lifetime of words left unsaid. Our connection was so tenuous I was afraid to utter anything but okay.

Soon after, I moved my mother into the nursing home and began to oversee her daily life. The irony of the apostate daughter becoming her mother's primary caretaker was not lost on me as I drove across town to visit her. Every Tuesday and Thursday we would go out to lunch—she loved the greasy French fries at Joe's Diner—then sit in the sun and doze or chat. Religion and rifts were never mentioned. And that routine continued for seven years: In that time she got to see her grandsons turn into young men, got to meet girlfriends and fiancés, got to hold her first great-grandchild.

Then one morning, the nursing home called. I rushed over but as I neared the facility the finality of death decelerated me to a slow motion tiptoe. She had passed smiling in her sleep. The ferocious woman who had so powerfully affected those around her now barely made a dent in the adjustable bed. I pulled up the shade and a shimmering light streamed through the room. I could not have articulated why I was weeping. Simply, in some strange way, I would miss her. *Have a blessed journey, Mom.*

Sitting at her bedside, I pictured going to Spain. There was no longer a tether holding me back. It was time; death put urgency to it. I went home and reserved a nonrefundable flight to Madrid. Smiling at the printed ticket, I noticed I was leaving on Mother's Day.

* * * *

NOW I WAS LYING on this floral quilt in a Spanish hotel. My growling stomach roused me from my reveries. The meal across the Atlantic consisted of suspiciously spongy chicken covered in unseasoned salsa; I had eaten the edges. I was starving. Quickly I rinsed out my hiking shirt then slipped on my sundress multi-tasking nightgown and went to the lobby to ask the soft-spoken concierge about dinner recommendations.

"Puerto Rican?" I asked, making sure I had heard him correctly.

"*Si, Señora*, it is the most authentic Spanish food around."

Don't ask if you are not going to follow the instructions, I admonished myself.

Following his directions, I walked several blocks and I found myself in a Puerto Rican dive being served by an Italian waiter what tasted like Jewish chicken soup. Steam caressed my face and the first spoonful filled my mouth with a savory buttery flavor that coursed through my body like the first sip of coffee in the morning. The waiter brought out a plate of sautéed pork slices and the luscious smell of this strictly un-kosher fare gave me a reminiscent twinge of guilt, while the accompanying French fries took me back to all those lunches with my mom. Finishing my meal with a large serving of flan, I licked the spoon and considered scraping the bowl with my finger.

Replete and reenergized, I felt like standing up and shouting: *Hell of a Mother's Day! I made it this far; bring on the rest!* I pulled out the travel plans from my waist pack and reviewed my arrangements for the next day: I needed to be in downtown Madrid early the following morning to catch a train to Pamplona, then a bus to Roncesvalles, my start on the Camino Frances. I left the restaurant and, having nothing to do, decided to purchase my subway ticket.

Walking into the balmy evening I knew I was far from home. San Francisco evenings are usually blanketed by chilly fog and here the warm air caressed my bare shoulders while the long, gentle dusk softened the night. I stopped at a ticket booth outside the Metro entrance.

"*Uno, por favor*," I said, trying to sound conversant. I couldn't understand a word of what the man said in response.

I breathed in the excitement of buying a one-way ticket. *I have no idea what I'm going to encounter. I'm simply going to head out and live through whatever happens.*

Wandering a bit through the mild evening I meandered to my hotel.

"Yes, I liked dinner very much. Thank you," I answered the concierge. Holding up my stub, I said, "And I got my ticket for the subway so I can get an early start tomorrow morning—"

He was chuckling.

"What's so funny?"

"*Señora*, this is not a train ticket." He pointed to the fingers crossed logo. "*Es un billete de lotería.*"

I started giggling with him. "Really? I got a lottery ticket?"

We burst into laughter, wiping our eyes between hoots. It was fun to see this seemingly staid man laughing so robustly. My amusement accompanied a sense of release. There was no way I could control this trip; my arms were up in the air for the rollercoaster ride.

"The ticket is yours. I hope you win a million Euros."

I truly hoped he would win. Along with the extra weight in my pack, I had shed a lot of what was unnecessary. I did not need more clothes or more money. A few years back I had encountered a weathered, homeless woman camped outside a church door. When I offered her five dollars she waved it off saying, "I have all I need." I had walked away wondering how anyone could refuse a few more dollars. Now as I propped my pack against the door, ready to head out in the morning, I could say the same: I have all I need. It was the beginning of my Camino.

2—Homeless

LET'S WALK TOGETHER. Put aside your bed, toilet, house, yard, shopping, gym, TV, phone, computer, and all the rest.
> *Are You kidding? I need those things.*
> *Do you?*
> *What would be left?*
> *Let's see.*

Was I going daft or was that actually God suggesting I put aside everything keeping my life together and walk five hundred miles across Spain? It sounded as mad as abandoning a life raft in a sea of white caps. Kneeling in St. Boniface Church, deep in the San Francisco Tenderloin, I grasped the pew in front of me and silently railed, *Why would I want to do that?*

I tried to ignore the celestial conversation as I had dismissed the Camino years ago when Reed had first mentioned it. He had come to fix my computer at a time my marriage was also on the blink. As we became friends he introduced me to the notion of walking distances and the Camino in particular.

"The trail is called The Way and it has been a pilgrimage since the ninth century. Popes, saints, and penitents have all walked it," Reed said.

"Hmm. Like who?"

"Like Saint Francis."

"Really? Imagine walking in the steps of a flesh-and-blood saint," I mused.

"Yes, and it goes through some beautiful areas of Spain," he continued, "foothills and forests, plains, cities and villages."

"And travelers camp on the side of the road?"

"In the past they relied on people living along the way for assistance; it was considered a blessing to help a pilgrim. Now there are lots of hostels as well as hotels and pensions."

"You mean youth hostels?"

"These are dorms where anybody can rent a bunk bed for one night. You share the bathrooms."

"You wouldn't catch me doing that."

"I'm planning on going again," Reed said. "The Camino is where I've been the happiest in my life."

I figured it was another peculiar trait of his. It certainly did not appeal to me. I had never gone backpacking, preferred a treadmill to trails, and was wedded to my own bed and toilet. There could not be a journey less suited to me.

But The Way kept circling around me like an annoying buzz—or a seductive whisper. Kneeling in this church, I felt an insistent tug to consider it.

The noon mass at St. Boniface ended; I blessed myself and got up. It was time to go to work. I needed to usher out the guests—as the homeless were called—and begin cleaning. Most of the guests were sleeping, tightly wrapped in their blankets like mummies lined on the pews. I woke them, hugged a few of the regulars, and reassured my avid reader friend that he would get another mystery novel next week. I said goodbye to the approximately hundred homeless who came to St. Boniface every day to seek respite from the streets.

Locking the massive carved doors, the staff and volunteers grabbed rags and bottles of disinfectant to start scrubbing the pews. The repetitive tasks, pick up garbage—spray and scrub—pick up garbage—spray and scrub, became a meditation in this huge, old, ornate church. As often happened, my mind circled back to the circumstances that had brought me to volunteer here.

A few years ago events had come together in perfect alignment. When the long estrangement from my mother ended with my becoming her caretaker, I took an early retirement then landed a great part-time job teaching dance. About the same time, I tumbled into a roaring romance. I balanced on the head of a pin of happiness and did not intend to budge.

Just as quickly the lovely construct shifted and crumbled. It started with having to put down my beloved black lab, my constant companion for thirteen years. A few days later, the affair ended the same morning as my job was frozen out of the state budget. Any one of the three would have been difficult but the triple, simultaneous hits packed a wallop. My world had collapsed.

At this bewildering juncture Father Seamus suggested I help out at a homeless shelter.

"Are you kidding?" I asked. "That's going to help?"

"Couldn't hurt."

It was beyond my comprehension how being with the homeless would assuage my loss of boyfriend, job, and dog. Numbly, somewhat reluctantly, I approached the Gubbio project in the San Francisco Tenderloin.

Gubbio is the name of the Italian city that had been terrorized by a wolf. The legend goes that St. Francis befriended the beast, transforming him into the city's protector. In San Francisco the wolf was the large homeless population roaming the streets after the shelters closed at 6:00 AM. Befriending took the form of "sacred rest," which meant opening St. Boniface Church and keeping it quiet, dim, and clean throughout the day. People went there to sleep or read or simply take refuge from the unpredictable din of the streets.

It took three fulltime staff and as many volunteers as possible to make *nothing* happen. We quietly patrolled the pews checking that no one was shooting up or eating or defecating, yet we often found needles, chicken bones, and worse. People came in tired, in need of rest, or hopped up on drugs, in need of a fight. We got trained in de-escalation and taught to keep our voices soft and threats real.

"Stop yelling or you will be banned for six months," I learned to say without blinking.

Dressed in carefully chosen faded jeans and a plain T-shirt, I helped out once a week. Volunteering had not come from any deep-seated sympathy for the homeless; it was an attempt to fill the vacuum in my life. And like many, I was squeamish of smells, germs, and bugs, and contemptuous of what looked like laziness. But as people got to know me they began to share their stories and I felt honored to accept the role of listener.

With his cultured voice and two college degrees, James taught me not to assume a lack of intelligence or education. He said he had made a conscious decision to live this "adventure" of homelessness and that he could change it at any time. He had worked for a marketing company in Denmark and often talked about going back.

"You speak Dutch?"

He looked disparagingly at me and said, "You mean Danish."

Another guest, George, scared me with his hair-trigger violence but deepened my understanding about the wounds of pain. Incarcerated on and off from an early age, he had been stabbed seventeen times and felt lucky to be alive. He was still seeking love in his life and was taking care of a heroin-addicted woman hoping it would work out.

Eva showed me which dumpsters contained the best food, her favorite being naan bread with yogurt.

Kevin made me aware how close art is to imbalance; I bought many of his paintings but they were too disturbing to display. I told Kevin that I could only talk to him for forty-five minutes at a time because after that I started seeing aliens too.

And Edward, my avid reader friend, touched me with the depth of his wisdom and love. He once mentioned, "I don't ever lend anyone money."

"How come?"

"If they need money I'll give them some but I won't lend it, because then I would expect it back."

I offered a receptive ear and was gifted with a change of heart. I began to listen, if not without judgment, at least with compassion. Each person at the Gubbio had a story that, given the right circumstances, could have been me. We were all searching for our place.

Talking with the homeless made me aware of my clenched grip on a meticulously ordered home. Living in my house for over forty years, I had married and divorced, raised my sons and said goodbye to them, without ever changing the arrangement of furniture. I knew I was compensating. My family had fled Egypt at the end of WWII when the creation of Israel made it dangerous for Jews to live in Arab countries. We were refugees for a while then landed in a newly developed suburb of Chicago, but I never felt at home there. So when I was able to settle in my own house with my husband and children, I rooted with a vengeance.

The homeless had their own routines and rootedness; many had secured sidewalk space that served as a postal address. A letter addressed to "Indian Joe, corner of Kearney and Market," arrived easily.

But what the homeless knew with certainty is that nothing is certain: We cannot hold on to anything. Their carts could be stolen or the cops could have a change of heart or they could be murdered in their sleep. They had the sea legs of a constantly shifting world. They taught me that if I accepted transience I had a chance of embracing presence.

I saw Leon on the street one foggy morning. He was stooped over the gutter wearing nothing but drooping sweatpants; his bare chest, feet, and peeking butt were glistening red from the damp cold. Finding what he was looking for he held up the smokable cigarette butt. He grinned broadly and shouted, "Isn't this a great day?"

Every Monday I walked the grim streets to help out at the Gubbio. Unnoticed and unsolicited, the possibility of stepping out of my rigid routine came into focus. The pull to the Camino—a cross between an itch and a yearning—felt supernatural because it was so strange. Yet the steps followed quite naturally: Losing my boyfriend, job, and dog—what I thought were the mainstays of my life—led me to open my heart to the homeless, and that connection loosened my grip on what I thought was security. By relinquishing the illusion of control, I was able to embrace the fantasy of freedom. The desire to walk began to grow. While Reed's encouragement pushed me from behind, the homeless pulled me ahead.

Despite the risk of sounding like a fanatic, I believe God used the events in my life to alter what I desired.

Come walk with me.
Really, Lord, just step out of everything I know?
You know me.

* * * *

SO I STARTED TRAINING, not Rocky-like sprints up stairs but leisurely hikes on nearby trails or rambles across town. A few hundred dollars put me in boots, a backpack, and floppy hat that tied under the chin, which my friends agreed looked absurd. The pack, filled with tuna cans and water bottles, weighed me down like a giant hand holding me in place and the hat made me feel fettered and hot. Worse than either was wielding the cumbersome walking poles my son gave me to "keep me safe."

One day, in full gear, I trudged past a strolling family when their three-year-old son pointed and laughed at me. The Japanese mother covered her mouth and apologized.

"I am so very sorry," she said, starting to giggle. "He says it's funny to see someone trying to ski on dirt."

I had to laugh with them. It felt very much like I was trying to ski on dirt. I could not say why I was preparing for this trip except that the Spanish trail kept beckoning. It was as if I wasn't choosing the Camino so much as the Camino was choosing me.

As my haphazard training plodded on, I discovered some new muscles and, unexpectedly, new perspectives. My tendency to schedule slackened. Leaving my car at the mechanic's I declined a ride and took the time to walk the few miles home. I meandered through different neighborhoods, stopped for tea at a café, and chatted with a teen holding his new puppy. My view of time moved toward the freewheeling, open perspective of a pilgrim. I had heard about this expansive sense of time from the homeless when they tried to explain why they did not want to go into public housing.

"I like being loose on the streets."

I got it. I liked that fleeting sensation of being loose in the world. But I also experienced something else the homeless talked about. I had not realized that wearing a full backpack in town signaled "street person" and now I was "one of them." People looked straight through me, which pierced more than an insult. It gave me a glimpse into the disparagement most homeless experience every day.

Once when I was resting on a bench outside a fashionable restaurant, a luncheon party gathered together after their meal. They were about my age and pleasant looking as they encircled my bench carelessly smoking and chatting. It was disconcerting being within their conversational circle yet invisible, like the seat I was on.

But I continued "skiing on dirt" until the day I whooshed into full flight. My mother's death had cut the last thread holding me back. Suddenly I was headed to Spain. And the sense of being without a home, both the freedom and estrangement, went with me. It accompanied me from my first step on the Camino to my last day in Madrid.

* * * *

MY FIRST DAY on the trail started when I walked out of the *albergue* in Roncesvalles and saw the sign *Santiago 780 km.* I thought *This is it! I'm beginning the walk!* However I couldn't find the trailhead and it took me quite a while to actually recognize the dim tree-arced entrance. When I did, I froze. Behind me stood all I knew: people, *albergue*, church, restaurants, stores, cars and buses. Before me was an empty forested path with no one on it. The magnitude hit me.

My God, I am homeless and alone. Everything I know is behind me. Are You with me?

The trail was silent.

This must be what it means to hope in things unseen. Here I go.

And I took my first step.

Like a snail carrying its home on its back, I struck out. Part of me felt free, with a swinging, unrestrained sense self-sufficiency, and part felt estranged knowing I wasn't connected to anyone. While no one was holding me back, no one was waiting for me ahead.

But what hit me most that first day was fear.

The Camino had an uncanny ability to confront its travelers with what we dreaded most. For some it was physical distress or lack of food; my terror was not having protection for the night.

The fear of not having shelter took me back to my family's horrific flight from Egypt, when we were in constant danger with no safe refuge. At three years old, I saw my parents' faces hollow and silent, powerless to prevent steely-eyed guards from ripping up our belongings. They detained us long enough that we missed our flight out of the country. Stranded with few possessions and no passports, we raced to the harbor and boarded a boat not knowing where it was headed. Even though we escaped, I have never been confident of a benevolent universe.

I faced that fear every day. By mid-afternoon terror tapes started gearing up: *There won't be a place so I'll have to walk on but it will be later and getting dark and even harder to get a place ...* There was no way to cut or quiet them. What I learned was that fear is not removed but replaced—I could out pray them. I cannot imagine what anyone thought observing me enter a village shouting Hail Marys at the top of my voice. That is one of the beauties of the Camino: Survival trumps self-consciousness.

* * * *

A COUPLE OF WEEKS into the journey, I walked through the arch of the medieval city of Burgos and fell in love with the place, captivated by the thousand-year-old gargoyles and sandcastle spires. A retired postman had helped me find the entrance to the city and, as he guided me through narrow cobblestone streets and spacious sunlit squares, he recounted stories of native son, El Cid. My guide dropped me off outside the municipal *albergue*, a slick four-story, 145-bed establishment within a grey stone monastic exterior. The Spanish are masters at fitting the old and new together: wonderful juxtapositions of worn stone and polished wood, antique arches and glass walls.

With the rest of the *peregrinos*, I waited in line, registered, and grasped my paper number. Lugging my pack up the stairs I saw that the beds were arranged in clusters of four, with each person assigned a cabinet for gear. Checking all the bunk groupings for my number it started to dawn on me—*it couldn't be*—that my bed was—*tell me it isn't so*—one of the two bunks stuck out—*no, no, no*—in the hallway. No little half-wall privacy, no shelf, no space—just out there on the well-traveled path to the toilets. It felt like I was squatting on the sidewalk.

Why did I get such a bad hand? This isn't fair. I know it's the luck of the draw but maybe they just didn't like me. Did I do something wrong? My internal rant sounded like many of the homeless who feel they have gotten a raw deal while also believing they brought about their own misfortune.

Double bunks had been added to one side of the hallway connecting the dormitory entrance with the cubicles housing toilets and showers; sinks dotted the other side. Pilgrims circled from their private cluster of beds, joking and chatting, brushing against my bed, on their way to the facilities. Normally I had no trouble stripping to my underwear to get cleaned up, but this hallway position felt so public I couldn't do it. Organizing myself for a shower seemed too daunting to attempt.

I decided to put off facing my plight. This postponement—like choosing to eat dessert first—was a strange reversal for me. Leaving the hostel, I started to wander around the intricate city. First I scared up a meal (no gourmet recipe can come close to the magnificence of plain bread and cheese on an empty stomach), and then a local resident treated me to tea as if I were a needy mendicant. At the end of day I met up with a fellow pilgrim for mass, tapas, and wine. Procrastinating with a second glass, I lingered, dreading the return to my squatting spot in the *albergue*.

Finally I staggered in unwashed, unpacked, unorganized, undisciplined. Needing privacy to regroup, I felt too exposed to put myself together. I did not want to deal with anything and wished I could disappear from everything. So I took an entire sleeping pill, which I had never done before. The sedative on top of the wine zoned me out so much I walked into a bathroom door and cut my nose. A river of blood overshadowed my dirty hair and grimy face. Just managing to unfurl my sleeping bag—brushing teeth and washing up seemed too formidable—I fell into bed with all my clothes on including my bra and, the grungiest part of me, my socks.

At 4:00 A.M. the morning traffic to the toilets started in full force. The four of us stashed in the hallway gave up on sleep, haphazardly stuffed our bags, and headed out. That is how I found myself hung-over, lurching, looking for signs to get out of the city in the pre-dawn darkness, stinking and bloody, ready to kill for a cup of any kind of caffeine. How often had I heard a homeless person say, "I was really stupid last night!"? If you have ever wondered how someone could let himself go that badly you would definitely have tsked-tsked at me. You would say, "There are facilities available; you need to pull yourself together, go to school, get a job, open a bank account." Of course it is true. But I understand how hard it is to care when life starts swirling like a river, impossible to grasp.

Trudging out of the city, the ancient cobblestones gave way to a gravel road and then a simple dirt path through the wide-open, endless *Meseta*. I slowly began to absorb the toxins and sleeplessness and to examine the experience of abandoning myself. I remembered Edward, at the Gubbio, saying he could not mess with washing clothes; he wore them until they stood, threw them away, and got new ones. I now had experienced how possible it is to ignore what we are supposed to mess with and will never again allow myself to disdain that the matted-hair-dumpster-diving homeless person could not be me. I will never again take privacy, or space, or quiet for granted.

Having started out so early, I reached Hornillos in time to get a corner bed with a little shelf on which to put my stuff. I scrubbed in a hot shower and hung my freshly washed clothes in the purifying sun.

Along with my clothes I hung out a plastic grocery bag. I thought how the Camino had honed not only my values but also what I found valuable. I was lucky to have wonderful high-tech high-functioning gear, but a simple plastic bag from the supermarket proved just as important. It turned out that when my full pack was strapped on, I could not reach my water bottles. Setting my pack down for every sip was not practical and asking for help was not always possible. The solution came a week into the walk: I realized I could put my water bottle in a plastic grocery bag and tie it to my waist strap. Not elegant but the best option I had. The first time I tried it the store's name, printed in green, rubbed off on my shirt. I found myself digging through discarded refuse for the perfect bag. Where had I seen that before? And when I found a plain white bag that was the correct size I treasured it like gold. Hadn't I seen the homeless carefully packing what looked like junk to me?

* * * *

THAT PLASTIC BAG holding my water bottle remained around my waist for the rest of the pilgrimage. It was extremely valuable until I finished walking; in Madrid it turned back to garbage and I simply threw it away. But I didn't know that another taste of homelessness awaited me.

I had planned for four tourist days in Madrid before flying home. Sitting on the night train from Santiago to the capital,

I realized I had changed: I had no problem sharing my water bottle with a complete stranger or popping a heart pill that had dropped onto a dirt-encrusted floor. It didn't bother me to use a toilet with five people waiting their turn and, using deep breathing techniques, I was able to get a little sleep with travelers talking and snoring around me. Although I had reservations at a hotel in Madrid, I had no particular plans for my stay there. Something had loosened.

As a treat for the end of the trip, I had reserved a room at a four-star hotel. Walking downtown from the train station, I caught sight of myself in the store windows. I saw a skinny, scruffy woman with grimy face, matted hair, and shoulders weighted down with a full backpack. My baggy pants with bulging pockets and a clothesline belt, my frayed shirt with a green smudge across the front, and my dusty hiking boots all looked strikingly out of place in this fashionable city. Gingerly stepping across the marble floor of Hotel Agumar I noticed meticulously groomed potted plants among the elegant leather seating arrangements. There were no flowers or colors; everything was a sophisticated grey or black with a polished sheen. I faced an incredulous desk clerk.

"*Buenos dias*," he said, looking warily at me.

"*Buenos dias*. I have a reservation here."

His short stature seemed to grow more erect. "You have a reservation?"

"Even a confirmation number."

He said he needed to "check" and left me standing there as he went into a back office. For half an hour.

"Very well," he mumbled on his return. "I assume you will want a room at the back. The very back is ... eh ... quiet."

"That's fine." I took the key and headed to the elevators; he had not called the porter.

My room faced a building but I didn't care in the least. I was staring at the bed: a double bed with ironed white cotton sheets, topped with a fluffy comforter and four gigantic pillows. I ran my fingers on the edge of the sheets then gasped at the full bathroom just for me. There were big white terrycloth towels and a counter full of little soaps and lotions, shampoo and conditioner. Looking in the shower I realized how much I had missed those little ledges on which to set the soap. Everything was gleaming clean and no one was waiting for a turn.

The next day I found a Thai shop that sold Spanish knockoffs and bought a white eyelet skirt and navy tank top. I located a beauty shop and had my hair cut into a short stand-up style and picked up a bit of make-up. I glanced at that reflective window again: Certainly I didn't look homeless anymore but neither did I look like the clench-fisted woman who had started this journey six weeks earlier. My clothes were suitable for a young woman, my gait was slower, and my hips swung more freely.

Scrubbed and skirted, sporting my sophisticated new haircut, I entered my hotel and waved hello to the desk clerk.

It was clear he had no recollection of seeing me before. Smiling he called out, "Ah, *buenas tardes, Señora.* How can I help you?"

3—The Sandal

PERCHED ON TOP of a spindly mountain, the village of Villamayor de Monjardín looked like a cartoon castle. All that was missing was Roadrunner beep-beeping while he raced up the two miles of backtracking path. It was a formidable climb for me, but there were no options.

My guidebook stated there was only one hostel in the town so, as the sun slid into mid-afternoon, my fear of not getting a place roared into high gear: *With only one albergue there is a much greater chance it could be full and the next town is miles away and ... What would I do?* The gut-wrenching message played over and over.

In an attempt to drown out the tape I recited Hail Marys counting my fingers like rosary beads. Completely separate from the clawing fear, an image of The Virgin took shape in my imagination. I had never been drawn to Marian devotion, probably because she is completely alien to the Jewish patriarchic tradition I grew up with. But I could see Mary, a young Jewish woman, baby due any minute, jostled on top of a donkey, with no bed in sight. Who was going to help her? There was only Joseph and he was busy trying to get them a room. Was her faith strong enough for her to sit calmly or was she panicked? Did she ever struggle with the existence of God like I do? She is called "blessed among women" yet lost everything imaginable. I had to agree with St. Teresa of

Avila who griped, "Lord, if You treat your friends like this no wonder You have so few."

While I was mulling over the pre-nativity scene, something caught my eye. It was a bit of greenish-grey peeking out of the rocks by the side of the trail. After two weeks on the Camino, I was still shocked and furious at how much litter was tossed aside and could whip up some hip-swinging indignation about people throwing garbage on their spiritual path. Attempting to pick up the trash proved as futile as bailing out a boat with holes, so I just shook my head in self-righteous annoyance.

As I got closer, I saw that this wasn't garbage but an intact sandal among the piles of loose rocks and dust. Probably it had dropped off of someone's backpack. Hikers often hooked their sandals to the outside straps of their packs—which was convenient but risky.

My internal debate began:

Should I pick it up to see if it belongs to someone in the village?

Are you kidding? You know it's awkward holding something while grasping the walking poles; you won't be able to lean your weight into them.

Sandals are crucial. Someone might be looking for it.

So what? The walk ahead is tough. Look, it's at least a couple of miles straight up. You can't do that while carrying something.

Somebody needs it.

Forget that. I am spent and have no energy to deal with that stupid sandal.

Think how wonderful it would be to find its mate.

What are the odds?

Like a mother dismissing her bickering children, I simply sighed and picked it up.

At first I tried hanging the shoe on my arm but it flapped against me, so I lined up the cross strap with the grip of my pole and was able to grasp both at the same time. It worked but the Velcro was scratchy and keeping it aligned against the handle was hard, making the strenuous climb feel steeper.

Panting up the last almost vertical steps, I stopped dead in my tracks. There in front of me was exactly what my terror tapes repeatedly described. Directly ahead, the *albergue* had strung a large banner across its entrance. In big red letters the placard announced: COMPLETO. FULL. There was no place for me. I had stepped into my nightmare. My God, what was I going to do? I stood there trying to breathe.

"My sandal!" A thin fortyish man with shoulder-length black hair came flying towards me, arms flung wide.

"My sandal!" he shouted again. Grabbing me by my shoulders he kissed me on both cheeks then twirled me around.

"La-de-da-dee—you brought my sandal," he sang while jumping a little jig. He gently extricated the treasure out of my clenched fist and waved it around, then gleefully danced a do-see-do with the friend next to him. Despite my no-place plight I beamed. It was worth having lugged it up there just to see his grinning face.

"*Gracias, gracias mi amiga.*" He hugged me again.

"*De nada,*" I lied, hugging him back.

"You are *peregrino*, no?" he concluded more than asked.

"Yes, but ..." I pointed to the banner above.

"Ah ..." he said as he turned to his friend. They spoke to each other in rapid fire Spanish.

It turns out the sandaled man had gotten into the shelter for the night but his friend, Pierro, had not. Consulting one another they came up with a plan. They knew of a pension in town and invited me to join. Putting their arms around my shoulders, the three of us sauntered into the village. I imagined a scene out of the Wizard of Oz.

The B&B we entered was light and airy with glossy parquet floors and enclosed gardens outside leaded-glass French doors. It smelled of furniture polish and flowers. The three of us looked like dusty vagabonds in this elegant setting as we tiptoed around peeking at the pristine bathroom that served the downstairs bedrooms.

"*Si*," the proprietor said, "I have room for 50 Euros." Pointing to Pierro and me: "There two beds. You share and cost half." He looked pleased with his idea.

Pierro did not speak English so my newly shod friend translated in a quick hand-gesticulating conversation. A leather-skinned man, Pierro looked to be about sixty with lines of life tooled deeply in his face. He peered at me and we shyly smiled at each other. This was not as risqué as it might seem. Many of the hostels on the Camino were mixed gender. My first few experiences with men and women together had me round-eyed timid but now it seemed almost natural.

"Sure," I said, striving for nonchalance.

As we went to the front to pay, another pilgrim came looking for a place.

"You have a bed?" he asked in a thick Italian accent.

I had noticed this striking middle-aged man on the trail because he used an umbrella for a walking stick, giving him a kind of Mary Poppins look. But his rugged six-foot frame and carved symmetrical face with the Roman nose was definitely masculine.

"My name is Claudio from *Italia*." His lilting voice almost sang as he turned to us and graced us with a sparkling smile.

The proprietor made a sweeping gesture with his arm, "Eh, *peregrinos* there is another of you. I have room with three beds. You share, just 17 Euros each." Why he was so intent on lowering our cost is not clear but we were now just a bit above what we would have paid at the hostel.

Pierro's dark brown eyes and Claudio's blue ones looked at me invitingly.

I only hesitated a moment. "Okay," I said. "But I am not sleeping in the middle."

We clambered in to view the large room with three beds lined up side-by-side, two beds and a rollaway. I took the farthest in, Claudio was next to me, and Pierro had the cot near the door. As we were setting up, I stroked the sparkling white, ironed sheets relishing the thought of slipping between them rather than crawling into my sleeping bag. We took turns showering, rinsed out our clothes, then linked elbows and walked to the only bar-café in town.

As we walked in, a spontaneous cheer erupted. Instantly we were enveloped in a crowd of pilgrims.

"There she is, the one who brought the sandal."

"Ah, *bueno*."

"Well done."

I felt my skin burn bright red as I received numerous kisses on my cheeks. Pointing to his feet, the man with the reunited shoes said, "Look!" and everyone applauded. We all got wine or beer and there were multiple toasts in a cacophony of languages interspersed with lots of laughter.

At one point a woman grabbed my arm. "There you are! Come, come with me. I want you to meet the wife of the man you are sleeping with." She pulled me to the other side of the room and I was introduced to Pierro's wife, who was the last person admitted into the shelter. The laughter turned ribald with double entendres.

"Ah, you are the one!" Pierro's wife said in mock fury, then she broke into a broad smile. "I'm so glad." She hugged me. "Thank you."

We drank and cheered and conversed as well as we could in broken bits of Italian, French, German, and English, raising our glasses often and loudly. After we had exhausted our toasts and consumed a hearty dinner, I said *ciao* to my companions. I wanted to explore the village, particularly the rough-hewn stone church at the edge of town. Walking through the twisted streets, the cobblestones were so uneven they arched my feet like a strenuous foot massage. The town seemed untouched by the last two centuries.

I approached the ancient church and was disappointed, though not surprised, to find it locked. As I turned away, the caretaker, a stocky man about my age, came by. He seemed pleased to open the chapel and show me the beautiful space, especially the ornate silver cross that was flanked by mirrors, extending its image to infinity. I thought how, like the mirrors reflecting the cross, one act leads to another then another:

Everything we do or not do ripples in concentric circles—possibly forever.

The sacristan helped me light a candle in front of a sculpture of Mary. This statue did not look like the usual plaster models with insipid expressions; this was a lovely mother, with a benevolent smile and a hint of whimsy. The caretaker stepped aside to give me a few minutes alone.

It is very strange for me to be in front of you. Mary, if you had anything to do with the way this day turned out, I am ever so grateful. Tonight I feel giddy with hope that things actually work for the best.

I got up and thanked the man. He nodded, took my shoulders, and gave me two almost chaste kisses on both cheeks.

Returning home to my roommates I found Claudio and Pierro sipping coffee in the living room. Our limited languages prevented any lengthy conversations but did not limit the warm bond we shared at that moment. We got ready for the night and quickly found ourselves luxuriating in real beds. Almost instantly I heard two baritone snores. Rather than being annoyed, the noise simply made me happy.

Lying there cozy and snug, I contemplated my day. What would have happened if I had I not picked up the sandal? It wouldn't have been earth shattering but the fellow who lost it would have been bereft. Most pilgrims toted only two pairs of shoes: hiking boots and sandals. Without the sandals it would have been difficult to air out his boots or wash his socks. Villages had few if any stores and, when he eventually got to a city, that type of sandal would be expensive to replace. Nothing life threatening, but enough to make him feel glum, and his somber mood would have affected his companions—just as his lighthearted dancing was also infectious.

Nestling deeper into the softness of the bed, I mulled: If I had walked past the sandal I never would have met its owner or his friend. Most likely I would have found the pension on my own but certainly not shared a room with anyone. Not meeting Pierro or Claudio, I would not have enjoyed their company or the mutual economy. Without the sandal I would never have experienced the raucous welcome, the cheery banter or kisses of camaraderie, the ribald jokes or heart-warming laughter. Had I not picked up the sandal I would never have gone to the chapel and thanked Mary.

I curled up and drifted off.

4—First Extraordinary Encounter: Eucharist

THE FIRST PROBLEM is what to call it and the second is convincing you I'm not crazy. Dreams can be visions, said C.S. Lewis in *That Hideous Strength*, but visions are never confused with dreams. This was clearly not a dream but I am loath to call it a vision. Visions are reserved for saints or mystics or at least the very devout. I am a pragmatic, somewhat ordinary, moderately Catholic, retired dance teacher, mother and grandmother. Let's simply call it an extraordinary encounter.

I was into my second week of walking and the morning started with three typical-for-the-Camino events.

As I was organizing my pack, preparing to leave the *albergue* at Santo Domingo, my seventeen-year-old friend from Germany swooped into my arms for a hug. He looked pale and limp with his shaggy, sandy colored hair matted to his head.

"Eh, I feel lousy," he moaned. "Do you have anything to offset a cold?"

Rummaging in my medication pouch, I found a vitamin packet. "Here you go." I handed him my last *Emergen-C*, fervently hoping I wouldn't need it. He immediately dumped the crystals into a bottle of water and chugged it down, waving thanks and goodbye.

That was foolishly magnanimous, I groused to myself.

As I laced my boots, a black-haired young woman with purple smudges under her reddened eyes approached me. In her thick Hungarian accent, she lamented, "I am so mad at myself. I expected this pilgrimage to give me wisdom and insight but all I do, day after day, is daydream. I could have these fantasies at home."

I could not fathom why she was confiding in me since we had barely spoken before. Looking up from my boot, I smiled at her and startled both of us by saying, "You're fighting your own thoughts so there's no room for anything else. Maybe insights start with self-acceptance."

Heavens, where did that come from? I would do well to heed my own counsel.

She looked a fraction less frantic. Giving her a quick hug goodbye I stepped out the door of the *albergue,* perched my pack on a bench, then swung it up without stressing my shoulders. When I first started the walk I had to squat in front of the pack, strap it on and awkwardly tilt up. I grinned, proud of how smoothly I maneuvered it now.

Just then Sasha, a woman I had met the day before, ambled out of the luxury hotel two doors down. She limped a bit as she came toward me and announced in her luscious southern drawl, "I simply cannot handle that ol' pack today. I just called a car t' carry it down the road t' the next *albergue.* They're holden' a spot for me."

Twin dragons of envy and indignation reared their ugly heads. Poison churned in my gut. I wanted a reserved bed too but without a phone that wasn't possible. Since I couldn't have it, I scoffed at her "Camino lite" travel style and what I deemed self-indulgence. I wanted to puff out my cheeks and shout that I was doing the real thing and she wasn't. Meanwhile I worried that her reserved spot affected my getting a place for the night. It felt like her good fortune detracted from mine.

It was your choice not to bring a phone and to carry your own pack, remember? And it looks like she needs it. I chided myself, but my resentment was far beyond rational.

"Well Buen Camino, then," I forced through clenched teeth.

"Oh yay-yes," she drawled. "Bueno Camino t' y'all."

Within a span of minutes, all my inconsistencies had come to the fore: generous and stingy, faith-filled and faithless, kind and mean, wise and stupid. Exactly me.

Because no café was open I walked the first few miles to Grañon tea-less and grumpy. I approached the small village like a horse smelling its feed. Up ahead I saw the beckoning outdoor plastic tables populated by friends enjoying breakfast. Intending to make a beeline straight for them, I felt a tug directing me to stop at the open church first. Somewhat reluctantly, I went in and knelt, asking for the strength to put God ahead of food and company. Lighting a candle, I prayed for all the people I held in my heart and who, at the same time, were holding me. Like an Escher painting, the disparate images of carrying while being carried seemed to fit together.

Then I got up and ran as fast as my nineteen-pound pack would let me to my sociable meal.

Carol, my Aussie friend, had finished eating and already left; Arlene, from Rhode Island, stayed to chat for a short while. The next city was Belorado, twelve miles up. Since we both preferred small, out of the way *albergues* we arranged to meet at a tiny shelter a couple of miles outside town. Given the difference in our paces, she would get there hours before me.

After my breakfast of tea with milk, bread and cheese, I took off through the beautiful abstract quilt of pastures. Fields of bright red poppies stitched next to vibrant goldenrod next to gray-green rye—all rippling as if hanging on a line. As I plodded on, it grew very hot. My wicking shirt hung limp with sweat and my hat seemed to offer little protection from the scorching sun. The terrain was wide open with rounding hills behind and a sloping valley before me. There was not a patch of shade in sight, no trees or houses or even fences to break up the endless fields.

Walking through the intense heat of the afternoon, I realized I was completely alone. I could see miles of path around but not one other pilgrim. And there were no farmers out, no cars or plows, no birds or rabbits. Even the breeze stopped stirring the grass. I had been humming the song *Jesus Remember Me* but it sounded out of place in this eerie, airless dome so I stopped. Other than my labored breathing and faint footsteps it was absolutely silent.

An image from early childhood came to mind. Even before Sputnik's launch caused a space flurry, I remembered picturing myself as a baby floating in the black void of the galaxy. I wore a little silver spacesuit with a thin lifeline protruding from the back, connecting me to my spaceship. Suspended and weightless, I saw myself floating in emptiness and felt not so much scared as utterly solitary.

I suspected that at least part of this feeling of disconnect came from leaving my home in Egypt at three years old, leaving my nurse and the box of buttons I played with and the painted sugar doll that sat on the top shelf of the kitchen. But I had no idea why these long ago memories were reappearing now.

My thoughts meandered to my dad who had suffered a stroke when I was a baby. I never knew him before he got sick. As we fled Egypt, every ounce of his strength went towards surviving his illness. I saw a tired old man with an uneven gait and slurred speech but I always fantasized that my father was straight and strong and powerful.

Thinking about my dad, I saw the lifeline that attached the baby to her spaceship get longer and thinner.

I thought about my mom turning her back on me when she found out I had become Catholic. I told myself that her actions came from what she knew, what she had grown up with, but that did not ease the pain. My feeling of being cast out remained.

The lifeline extended even farther and became as flimsy as sewing thread. My sense of aloneness deepened in the heavy silence. The only sounds I heard were my soft footsteps on the baked dirt path.

Step—step—

Someone was alongside me. I could feel the weight of footsteps and gentle warmth radiating from a presence. The comforting heat—very different from the searing sun of the day—was a lot like the closeness of a friend. I didn't see anything but I knew Who walked beside me.

Jesus told me He was holding that baby. He always had been and always would be holding me.

I thought for a moment, then in my normal tactless manner responded that it was hard to believe. I told the Lord, "I don't feel held and never have. Can't even imagine it." My breath caught at my own brazenness.

He didn't speak or scold but a glow of light diffused around me and I saw—I clearly saw Jesus' hands—large and caring—His cupped hands, one within the other, cradling that little spacesuited baby—holding me gently and carefully, specially and specifically.

I stopped dead. It was a spectacular image filling the entire dome of the sky. What was even more amazing was that the Lord held me in His palm as His Eucharist. *How could this be? How preposterous! How presumptuous! How could I dare to even imagine this?*

"Lord, how could it be? You are the Eucharist. You are our food, our manna from heaven. I can't be Your Eucharist."

The answer was quiet but clear, "You are part of me."

"I am nourishing to You?"

"You are my precious child. You feed me."

"Me?"

The surrounding emptiness was filled with universe-sized hands holding me as Communion. I was embraced exactly as I was, with all my discord, flaws and failings. I gaped in awe. As I slowly turned to take it all in, I beheld the world in a totally different way: The day that had been stifling and oppressive was now filled with vibrant energy. Where I had felt detached and alone I now felt connected to everything. It was an unfathomable mystery. All was held in love.

My heart expanded as I stood round-eyed in word-less, thought-less wonder.

Then my mind entered the scene and the image evaporated. I tried to understand how the contradictory ideas of consuming and being consumed fit together. Thinking back to my morning stop in church, I remembered how I carry the people who love me while, at the same time, am carried by them. It was the same Escher-like shift of perspective.

Niggling thoughts that this was a heat hallucination or that my wounded psyche made it up had not snaked into my consciousness yet. Poised by myself on that path, I knew with utter certainty that I held the Lord in my hands while he held me in His. I also knew that just as I was tenderly cradled, so was every single, no-matter-what person in the world.

Tears of gratitude washed my face as I continued blindly down the trail. "Lord, if this vision is the reason You called me to the Camino, it is enough. Like the Jewish Passover song of thanks, *Dayenu*, 'It would have been enough. For this we are grateful.' If I were to go home today it would be more than sufficient. I feel I could be sustained by this vision for the rest of my life. Thank You."

But like any meal, even those so complete we think we will never want to eat again, after a few hours we get hungry. I could see the *albergue* in the distance, nestled in a grove of trees a half-mile off trail. Despite my gratitude for this most beautiful vision, my fear of not getting a place reared its ugly head again. It was like the morning incongruities. Joyfully accepting God's kindness and compassion sat uneasily next to skepticism and doubt. Having been given heaven I was still battling my own hell.

I can't expect the Lord to help me get a place when He's already given me this incredible vision. Now I'm going to walk an extra half-mile off trail to get to this hostel and it's going to be full and then I'll have to walk back plus another two miles to town ...

The next thing I knew I was entering the rose covered gate of a lovely *albergue*. Lush gardens surrounded the whitewashed tile-roofed house. The shelter was one wing of a rambling family home. I heard children running and laughing in the family's quarters and smelled something garlicky simmering in the kitchen.

When I was shown my assigned bed in a large dormitory I froze in disbelief. There were only two other guests in that spacious room, Carol and Arlene. I was encircled by affection. The abundance of gifts seemed too much for me, and tears spilled out. I couldn't stop sobbing. My friends left the room to give me privacy. Setting down my pack, I leaned against the cool metal bunk frame. The idea of being so lovingly cared for by God was beyond my grasp; accepting that possibility, if only for a moment, overwhelmed me. I slobbered through my bandana, all the toilet paper in my pocket, and my shirt.

When I was spent, I set up my gear, took a shower, and joined the congenial group in the garden under the cherry tree. My nose was plugged and my eyes gritty from crying but I felt light and content. There were about a dozen pilgrims seated on benches and chairs around the yard, all telling trail stories, laughing and enjoying one another's company. Pots of colorful flowers abounded, dogs and chickens wandered among us. It felt homey and welcoming.

I didn't say much but I couldn't stop beaming. My two friends looked at me with concern and curiosity. I nodded to let them know I was fine, feeling awash with love for them, for our group, for our lovely hosts. In that moment I rested in the image of being held.

Ordering two bottles of wine, I asked the other pilgrims to share a toast. We raised our glasses.

"To the gifts of the Camino," I said.

"Hear, hear."

I did not mention that the wine was accompanying the Divine Host. We finished both bottles and ordered two more.

5—Signs

LOTS OF PEOPLE bring navigational systems on the Camino but they don't need to, the trail is well marked.

At Roncesvalles—the Spanish start of the Camino Frances—I had my picture taken with the large placard, *Santiago 790 km*. Then I got mixed up, went the wrong way, and circled the entire *albergue* complex before finally heading out.

The path might be well marked but you have to spot the signs.

Directions could come from billboards, concrete posts, and painted walls, but mostly we followed little yellow arrows. A priest named Father Stampede started this mission a hundred years ago in an effort to—I can't resist—herd pilgrims. Now the arrows are found everywhere: on trees, traffic poles, buildings, fences, rocks, or painted on the road. Sometimes the markers are not drawn but fashioned out of sticks or small rocks; my cynicism, after forty-plus years of teaching, made me pause at the possibilities for a mischievous child. These cheery arrows guide and encourage pilgrims along the entire trail, which is why souvenir shops are chock full of arrow pins (one on my hat), shirts, hats, ties, bags, scarves, jewelry, mugs, tiles, and trivets.

It's like a secret sign. Walk down any street in the world wearing city clothes, like heels and a dress, then add a little yellow arrow to your scarf or lapel and watch what happens.

Most likely someone will nod and call out, "Buen Camino." It makes me wonder what other signals, knowingly or not, we send out.

Throughout the journey I was careful to follow all instructions, but the signs were sometimes obscure. Camino arrows could look a lot like yellow tree fungus, which got me thinking how often in my life I might have confused a bunch of mold for a sign from God—and the other way around. Plus the arrows were rarely located at the center of intersections; they were more likely found on a wire above the path or embedded in the pavement or a ways down the road. Desperately searching for guidance usually did not work. The easiest way to spot a sign was with relaxed eyes and a gentle expectant sweep of the area.

Despite my efforts to stay on track, I was amazed to see a lady huffing up a hill after me, waving her arms and shouting, "*Peregrino*, you are not on the path." Another time a bartender climbed out the window of his café to grab me and yell, "No, no, wrong way!" The cynic whispered, "Why would they care?" but the rest of me bellowed, "Thanks for keeping me on course!"

Once while hiking on a gravelly path under a freeway system, I realized I had not seen a sign for a while. Every pilgrim avoids backtracking but a growing apprehension that I had gotten off track made me retrace a mile until I ran into another traveler. The smiling young man, dressed in a red bandana and fringed vest, reminded me of Berkeley in the sixties.

"All good," he said with an otherworldly smile. "You are on the way." Then he held up his fingers in a peace sign. I believe I actually returned the gesture. Re-trudging the same steps for the third time, I realized that if I had kept going another ten feet I would have seen the clearly marked arrow. It's hard to know when to hold on and when to cut loose.

One time I walked without markers. My guidebook described the entrance into Burgos as industrial, trafficked, and generally unpleasant. The author suggested an alternate, "less marked" trail that went through a park—all we had to do is follow the river. How hard could it be to follow a river?

I entered the enormous city park, reminiscent of Golden Gate or Central Park on either coast, and found the path not less marked but not marked at all. However the river was in plain sight and there was a little footpath alongside—it seemed easy. As I walked I reveled in the lovely dappled light and green lawns and the lapping sound of a lazy waterway. Briefly wondering why there were no other pilgrims, I congratulated myself on choosing this alternate route. Then I came to an abrupt stop. Up ahead the waterway divided in two: The larger branch seemed to backtrack while the smaller stream headed in the direction I had been traveling. What river do I follow? There was no sign of any sort.

A large, smooth boulder marked the split between the two rivulets. It was early in what was meant to be an easy hiking day so I serenely took off my pack, climbed on top of the rock and waited for directions. If anyone had told me at the start of my journey that I would sit on a rock expecting instructions to appear I would have rollicked in laughter. *Yeah, and wave some crystals while tapping my divining stick.* Yet here I was.

Pulling out my stash of nuts, I munched on a handful and began thinking about my decision to come on the Camino. I saw that among the influences leading me here was my search for a sign. My life felt like it had hit empty and was sputtering. I was headed toward old age and couldn't fool myself into thinking I was midway. Though I felt thirty, this vaguely familiar old lady kept glancing at me from the mirror. It was disorienting. It wasn't simply the wrinkles and lowered stamina, the reduced speed and slower recovery time. It was the waning number of possibilities: I was never going to climb Yosemite's Half Dome, never have a "big job" or be a mainstream performer.

Most of the time I felt grateful for what I did have, but—although it seemed greedy—there was a void, a sense of emptiness and longing that leached my well-being. Besides, I wasn't sure my discontent could be remedied in this world.

Would another romance or published book fill me up? Could this five-hundred-mile walk change anything but muscle tone?

A divine arrow would help. I wanted a sign that I was part of a bigger design, that I was a thread in some intended and intricate universe-sized tapestry. If I were part of something enormous and eternal, my speck of a life would be significant.

I was lost in thought when a woman walked by. She was wearing a calf-length, baby blue, suede coat appropriate for opening night at the opera and torn tennis shoes ready for the garbage bin. I asked her if she knew which way I should go to get to Burgos.

She pointed to the smaller stream and, in a strong British accent, declared authoritatively, "You'll want to go that way."

"Thanks," I said offering her some nuts. I hoisted my pack and headed the way she had indicated.

A few minutes later she came running after me. "No, no, go the other way."

I felt like Alice in Wonderland following these wacky directions and my shoulders sagged with lack of confidence. But I couldn't think of anything else to do; so I switched to the opposite path and hoped for the best.

After a few miles I got stuck again. I was blocked from skirting the river by a large construction site, which required a detour along meandering park trails. Then I couldn't find the river again, got totally turned around, and had no idea in which direction I needed to go. Worse, in all that time I never saw another pilgrim, not one peering-over-the-head backpack. Though it was a cool day, sweat started trickling through my hair and down the front of my shirt, and my heart and breathing began speeding up despite my attempt to control them. Why, why, why, I badgered myself, had I strayed from the straight and arrowed?

Working hard to calm myself, I approached a group of picnickers and, in my broken Spanish, found out the correct path to Burgos. I traipsed off and after a while was delighted to see the city through a grove of trees—except it was impossible to get there. C.S. Lewis talks about being close but not near, like being on a mountain peak fairly close to another peak but an enormous walking distance from it. The city was visible ahead, but I could not fathom how to forge the river, then scale the fence, highway, and fortress walls.

Haven't I often felt left out and separate—the immigrant looking in? Now I'm stuck in this labyrinth with the city in sight but I'm outside and helpless. Lord, are You with me?

Tears started to seep out the corners of my eyes.

Crossing a little wooden bridge, I stopped to blink away the tears and watch the swirling eddies below. My mind whirled back half a century to a highway bridge where I had also felt helpless: I had been driving on a four-lane Chicago freeway when a sudden slowdown caused me to pound too hard on my brake pedal and lock it. My car skidded across all the lanes of jam-packed, eighty-miles-an-hour traffic, while trucks and cars slammed into me and propelled me toward an overpass. At the last minute I yanked sharply on the steering wheel and managed to turn the car away from the precipice.

Now leaning on this rail overlooking a gurgling stream, my muscles clenched as I remembered my desperation. My car had spun back across the freeway, batted right and left by other vehicles, and landed on the center divide. There was a sickening crash of metal hitting concrete. Black smoke spewed from the engine and the car abruptly tilted as a wheel rolled off. My vehicle was battered into a trapezoid shape with the front passenger and back seats completely crushed. Anyone sitting there would have been killed. I sat dazed for a minute then slowly tested the driver's door. It creaked open unevenly. Unfolding my legs, I checked for gashes or breaks while tentatively stepping out of the automobile. There was not one bruise or scratch on me.

Sirens screeched in the distance but before any of the emergency vehicles arrived I stood alone on the small divide of a gigantic freeway next to a crumpled heap of metal. Even though I did not have a spiritual practice then, I knew this was no ordinary event. The possibility of being touched by the supernatural filled me with awe: *I shouldn't be standing here. Someone wants me alive.*

That car accident happened decades ago and through the years I have tried to keep the wonder alive in my heart: *Someone. Wants. Me. Alive.*

Wasn't it a miracle? Shouldn't that sign sustain me forever?

"*Señora*, do you speak French or English?"

I jerked my head to the side, startled to find a diminutive man wearing a white and blue windbreaker. He was standing alongside me but I had not seen him materialize. I would have been taken aback except that his expression was so open and friendly he looked like a fairy-tale elf.

"*Oui*," I replied.

He said he wanted to practice these languages and asked if he could accompany me on the path. I looked at him in astonishment, then relief washed over me and the held-in tears broke free. He pretended not to notice.

We walked together, chatting in a mixture of French and English with a dash of Spanish. My companion informed me he was a native of Burgos, recently retired from the postal service, and that he used his newfound time to hike in the park and polish the languages he had learned in school. We ambled through meadows and a forested area, and then the parkland merged into the front lawn of a visitor center advertising the Atapuerca Caves, home of the earliest human remains. We giggled as we took silly photographs of each other standing among the statues of a prehistoric family. Then I left him holding my backpack and poles as I ran to use the porta-potty.

My guide led me through the ornate, high-arched entrance to the city and down the twisted streets of Burgos. He pointed out major landmarks while recounting the rich history embedded in this storybook medieval town, especially the exploits of native son, El Cid. At an outdoor café we stopped to chat with several of his acquaintances who looked at me warily until they realized I had no designs on their friend. My lovely guide dropped me off in the line outside the *albergue* and hugged me warmly. I have a picture of him but we never exchanged names.

Waiting in line, I smiled thinking about my entrance into the city. *Lord, I am a fish swimming around praying for water. I was hoping for a little arrow and You sent me an angel. How can I thank You?*

Looking up at the spires of the Burgos Cathedral, I suspected I would not end my pilgrimage filled with unshakeable faith. But I was content with signs rather than certainty. The arrows pointed to the divine; it was my choice to follow.

6—Pockets

THERE IS A MOVIE about pilgrims on the Camino that is very true to life except for one thing: The lead actress is wearing snazzy skin-tight jeans. It would never happen. No pilgrim wears jeans, certainly not tight ones. They're too hot, too heavy, too constraining, and if they got wet you'd be sunk. More importantly there's no room to fill the pockets, which are almost as necessary as the pack. The hiking pants I wore were high-tech, zip-into-shorts, microfiber, dust-tinted marvels—with seven pockets. One escaped notice until I got home and one was a secret mesh pouch accessible only by pulling the pants down. I used the other five.

Left Hip

My left side pocket held the all-important toilet paper: napkins, Kleenex, paper towels, tissue. It was iffy to find a bathroom on the Camino and improbable it would include paper. Only half the bars and restaurants had some kind of wipe, *albergue* toilets started out with paper but generally ran out, and of course bushes ...

When I first started walking the Camino I was embarrassed to be seen leaving the trail for a clump of bushes. I would walk miles in growing discomfort looking for the perfect hide-a-way coinciding with the least number of spectators to witness my detour off trail.

By the end it was a different story. I was behind a shoulder-high bush when the Party Pilgrims came along. They were a group of early forty's German men who were drinking their way across Spain. When they saw my head peeking above the shrub, they waved and called out noisily, "Oh, there's Sheila peepeeing behind a bush. Hi there."

I waved back, laughing and joking with them with hardly a hint of embarrassment.

Prickly bar napkins, rough towels, and of course tissues were all prized and ferreted away in my pocket. The concerns of the Camino were concrete and immediate. Elimination, thirst, pain, and food vied for the spotlight. Reflection, memory and musing occurred after the basics were attended to—it is impossible to pray when you need to pee.

After returning home, I heard friends say they wouldn't be caught dead going in the bushes. But the Camino will have its way: You do what you have to.

Right Hip

The Camino tends to erase all sense of what is flattering or fashionable (except for the end of the trail where there is an astonishing collection of outfits, from matching spandex workout gear, to full blown brown-wool pilgrim costumes, to loin cloths combined with self-flagellating whips) so it did not bother me that the toilet paper bulge in my left pocket was matched by a hippy lump in my right: watch, glasses, and camera.

It was driving rain the day I walked into Pamplona. As I leapt over a small-lake puddle, the sleeve of my rain jacket caught on my watchband and I felt it snap, hurling my watch into the mud. *Oh great, I'm soaked and miserable and definitely not going to finish the ten miles I planned for today, and now my watch is gone. Where will I find another one here?*

Retrieving the timepiece from the puddle, I found it miraculously still worked. So I threw the broken band away and tucked the watch face in my pocket. That started a new dialogue with time.

Being a time-oriented person, I have always been aware of the hour and allotted lots of just-in-case minutes, which usually made me early for everything.

"Mom, you got us to soccer twenty minutes before practice again," my kids would whine.

"Think of it as transition time."

I was attached to my simple, sturdy analog watch and every few years replaced it with an identical model. With the aid of that timepiece I was able to juggle home, children, and fulltime work. I could end a dance class in precisely forty-three minutes, if that was needed, and in almost half a century of teaching I was never late. I managed time more than lived it.

With the watch face deep in my pocket, I slowly began to realize what a gift it was not being able to check it easily. I would have allowed time to direct my pilgrimage: *Oh I should have gotten there by now ... Gee I haven't eaten in six hours ... I've walked four hours so I should rest.* Now I had to sense other cues. Guidebooks talk about resting and refueling every couple of hours, but I found that after a small breakfast, I generally liked a steady pace with few breaks until I got to my destination village. It wasn't better or worse; it was just what worked best for me. And I would never have discovered my preference if I had kept track of the time.

The same week I broke my watch, one lens of my reading glasses popped out, forcing me to peer through the other side. Not having workable glasses cemented the fact I had nothing to read except my guidebook. (The romance novel I had brought for the plane was long gone.) Even though I normally fill a grocery bag with library books and often fall asleep with a volume on my chest, I chose to eliminate reading from this journey. The main impetus was weight, since every ounce rested on my shoulders, but I also thought it might be healthy to go on the wagon from my literary escape. Like an addict without her fix, this left me with periods of intense longing. Breaking from books forced me to be still and face what was happening without running away, which was probably good for my character and hard on my nerves. Like my hidden watch, it was a gift that took time to appreciate.

At the top of that right pocket, wedged above the watch and glasses, was my camera. Like everyone else I had taken it to record my journey; I had not expected the camera to generate its own experiences, especially one I am reluctant to tell. Previous to the pilgrimage I had only used a film camera, but days before leaving I realized there was no room for canisters and I quickly bought a simple, inexpensive digital model. This is where the embarrassment comes in. I am so technologically deficient I needed my son to give me a cursory lesson on how to work it—which he did. But he did not mention charging it, and being clueless, I left without a line. Of course within a week it was dead. Another pilgrim—looking at me as if I had materialized from another planet—spoke slowly and deliberately as he informed me I required a charger.

At breakfast the next morning I casually mentioned what I needed to the café owner. He said he had a charger and would sell it to me for 7 Euro. I was ecstatic. Now I would not have to hunt down an electronics store in the next city. I thanked him profusely, paid, and headed out.

He called me back. I was alarmed that he might have changed his mind about selling it to me because he was looking down at his shuffling feet.

"Uh, I did not ... um ... it did not cost me 7 Euro for the charger."

"Yes?"

"It only cost 2. I feel bad charging you more."

I looked at him in amazement. Standing before me was pure conscience. He felt ashamed taking advantage of a pilgrim.

Grasping his arm, I said, "Please don't feel bad. You've done me a huge favor and I would have gladly paid more. I still thank you very much."

His eyes welled up in relief. "I want to give you a gift."

I protested vehemently but he handed me a little brown flower-painted souvenir vase, typical of the region. It was fragile and weighed about a half a pound. I had ruthlessly rid my pack of excess, refusing to carry a book, film, eye make-up, and full clothesline, yet now I tenderly wrapped the present in one of my gloves and cradled it in the top pouch of my pack.

Left, Back and Front

When I first got my pilgrim passport I nonchalantly stuffed it in my back pocket with the ATM and store receipts. The document is a stamped record of every *albergue* visited and, in Santiago, the pilgrim office would scrutinize it to see if I qualified for a certificate of completion. I scoffed at the whole idea of pilgrim passports and certificates: It smacked of gold stars and sticker charts.

Time and distance wore down my disparagement so that, midway through my journey, I found I had unwittingly transferred my pilgrim passport to the double-zipped, cable waist pack holding my U.S. passport and money. The credential had become valuable to me.

It is easy to ridicule faith and spiritual journeys—even one's own. They can appear hokey and naïve. My mother and siblings rejected me for embracing Christianity but any pursuit of faith distanced me from my worldly friends. They saw me as gullible and simpleminded.

"You really believe he was God?" asked a long-standing, college friend.

"Well, yes, most of the time I do."

"And he ... walked on water?"

"Why not?"

I remember her look of alarm and superiority. Holding on to my own view took effort. We found conversation increasingly difficult and eventually our friendship drifted apart.

It is perfectly acceptable these days to talk about the universe granting this or that wish, to study the courses of energy and laws of attraction, to pray to higher powers, guardian angels, and ancestors. Plenty of people invoke parking gods to help them find a spot and no one blinks at *OMG* as an exclamation. Dare to mention *God* or *Jesus* and people bristle. I had accepted both.

The trouble is that I swallowed their antagonism. The piercing rejection from family and friends became my own. *You are an apostate betraying your heritage. You are no better than a Nazi and have forsaken every Jew who died for their beliefs. How can you believe all that mumbo-jumbo?* Those are my tapes. I have had to fight my own disownment by revisiting the steps that led me to my beliefs.

Moving the pilgrim passport to a place of value was a subtle shift within myself. It was a tiny, hesitant step toward fully embracing my perceptions and choices.

While the pilgrim passport moved from my back pocket to the waist pack, the three pebbles in the left front pocket were dropped along the way. The stones were brought from home and placed at crosses throughout the pilgrimage; the ritual is intended to release fears and worries. Leaving stones on gravesites is also a Jewish tradition meant to honor the memory of the deceased. Even though I had converted, I hoped the Jewish martyrs would accept my reverence.

On top of the spiritually significant stones, I squeezed in lip balm, toothpicks, and a faded pink bandana, which served as a handkerchief (saving that valued toilet paper), facecloth, cold compress, towel, bandage, fly swatter, tote, clean-up rag, and headscarf.

Right Front Pocket

One pocket remained. Different from the rest, the right-front compartment had a zipper as well as a Velcro flap—the Fort Knox of pockets. It was perfect for my ultimate treasures.

Stone:

At the *albergue* in Ponferrada, I met a Buddhist nun, strikingly beautiful with her shaved head and brown robe. I had bumped into her and her companion at the entrance door while I happened to be holding a bag of my prized hazelnuts.

Extending the bag, I asked, "Would you like some?"

The nun smiled broadly while her friend said a bit sternly, "We eat two meals a day and no snacks."

"Oh. Sorry."

The next morning this gentle looking religious approached me and bowed; with sparkling eyes, she silently offered me a single grape. I accepted it with a bow of my own and popped it in my mouth. She then reached into the pocket of her robe and handed me a little stone about the size of a thumbprint. On one side of the smooth, flat, green-gray oval she had painted delicate gold leaves that appeared to emanate from the stone itself. On the other side she had drawn three Chinese characters, which her companion explained represent an extension of peace. It is a stunning miniature. We both bowed.

How could she know? Did she have special powers that saw my love of rocks? Could she guess that every jacket I own contains a smooth stone in the right hand pocket? Working hard to stay ceremoniously composed, I wanted to sit down and sob. I could not fathom why she had selected me, why she had chosen an old Jewish-Catholic stone-lover to receive her labor and wishes. Feeling awed and grateful I bowed low and held it for a few seconds, then slipped the stone in my pocket.

A Pendant:

Nestled next to the stone is a lightweight pendant of pilgrim St. James, arms open in welcome. I am not a devotee of James because he is also portrayed as a violent Moor slayer and I simply do not see how such violence fits in with a gentle savior. This image is of an embracing saint and it was a gift of openhanded generosity.

I went into a bar to use the toilet, expecting to be told it was for customers only—or at least glared at. The journey was sprinkled with people who valued our trek as a spiritual undertaking but just as many were fed up with demanding pilgrims. Almost everyone saw us as an opportunity to make a buck.

"Welcome, *peregrino*, come, come in, the toilet is right in back. And I have something for you," the bartender called out.

I was stunned. "Thanks," I said, warily heading to the rear.

When I returned, a smile crinkled his entire face as he handed me the pendant of a welcoming St. James on a string. This anonymous random kindness, with no thought of return, softened and sweetened me.

"This is so lovely. Will you help me put it on? I cannot thank you enough," I gushed.

Like meanness, kindness can grow like a seed. It reminded me of the little pendants—"seeds" she called them— that Mother Theresa handed out not knowing which would take root. A neighbor of mine got a pendant from Mother Theresa and although he would have described himself as nonreligious, it never left his neck; now he has passed away and the pendant is securely around his wife's neck.

I wore the memento for a few days but the cord became annoying so I transferred it to my pocket of treasures. Later in my trip I met a fellow wearing one of these bar pendants. When I showed him mine his face drooped in disappointment.

"I thought I was the only one to get it," he whined.

"I think they are meant for everybody."

A Star:

The pendant's white cotton string became tangled with a small cardboard star. The star looks painted by a child but cut by a surgeon. Augustinian sisters gave it to me.

I had debated whether to stay in this town or the next; like everyone else I read my guidebook meticulously, figuring out what distance seemed appropriate and which *albergue* description sounded best. Municipal shelters were usually new, big, clean, and noisy while private hostels were more expensive, older, and occasionally dirty. It all came down to the luck of the draw—literally what *albergue* drew me.

In Carrión I found myself pulled to the convent-run *Albergue Maria*. It turned out to be a true refuge with the habited sisters welcoming us as one of their own. They offered the pilgrims an evening blessing after mass. About ten of the fifty guests gathered in an alcove filled with colorful pillows, underneath a rounded staircase of beautifully polished wood. The rest of those staying were tramping up and down the stairs, looking askance at us and whispering loudly.

"What are they doing down there?"

"Some kind of nunny thing."

"Geez."

"Can you imagine wearing those long black dresses in this heat?"

The sisters sang with sweet joyful voices. Then, after blessing us, they gave us the stars they had made to symbolize our part in a larger, cosmic design. Overwhelmed by their open kindness, I started quietly crying. One of the sisters hugged me tight and said,

"You never, ever, walk alone. We will pray for you."

Messages:

Three slips of paper joined my treasure trove. One is a business card from a towering, California hunk with whom I spent a most enjoyable afternoon and evening; though I never saw him again I kept his card. The other two scraps of paper are messages, one from Helmut and one from Gandhi.

I bumped into Helmut early on the trail. At that point in the walk I had not figured out how to fasten a bottle so I could reach it without taking off my pack. I saw a sandy haired, fiftyish fellow (who turned out to be Helmut) and asked him to help me reach my water bottle. Then I brazenly requested he wait a moment so he could put it back.

"That's it then!" he growled in a German accent.

"Thanks so much," I said with a smile.

The next day I ran into Helmut again at a tiny *albergue* nestled in the ruins of St. Anton's ancient monastery-hospital. The crumbling stone walls of the ruins had tufts of grass growing in the cracks and open windows that framed the neighboring fields—the scene was so magnificent it looked like a fake Hollywood set or the background of a cheesy Renaissance painting.

I bought Helmut a coke from the startlingly incongruous vending machine tucked into the ancient stone with an electrical line hooked up to the neighboring farmer's generator. He then showed me how to drink from the traditional pilgrim jug. I did not master the throw-it-in-the-back-of-your-mouth technique and ended up spilling half a pitcher of water down my front.

"That's it then," I laughed. And we became friends.

Since there was no electricity or showers, the small group of pilgrims staying at St. Anton's washed up in candlelight and spent the evening singing while watching a downpour of rain. We bonded together and the next day joined our *hospitalera* at a mass in a nearby convent. (Being such a slow walker I got to the convent later than the rest. I went in the wrong door and startled a half-dressed African man who turned out to be the priest. "No worries," he whispered later handing me Communion.) As we were leaving, our host suggested we might enjoy staying at the hostel run by her fiancé for our next stop. She offered to call to let him know we were coming. No electricity at these two hostels but everyone had cell phones. We all agreed and headed out to St. Nicolas.

When I reached that lovely 12th century church-turned-*albergue*, all the beds were taken. The others in our group had been the last in. Since the hostel had closed for siesta I sat outside debating what to do. I could wait and see if the previous *hospitalera* had called and they might be able to squeeze me in, or I could immediately head out for the next town. Logic voted for the latter and I opted for the former. Resting on a promise and a prayer was not typical of me; my fear was greatly affronted and circled my head like squawking crows.

Meanwhile Helmut had been dealing with his own problem: He had left his wallet in a café in the previous village and was waiting for a taxi to deliver it. We sat next to each other on a bench quietly immersed in our own thoughts. Suddenly Helmut jumped up and grabbed my shoulders.

"I am giving you my place," he announced. This was an unheard of gift.

"I can't accept that."

"Yes, it is for you. When the taxi comes I will go to a hotel."

Of course I burst into tears.

It turned out that the previous *hospitalera* had called and they had found a place for me; we both could have stayed. That did not lessen the magnitude of the gift nor change Helmut's decision. As he climbed into the cab he handed me a folded slip of paper, directing me to read it later that evening.

"That's it then?" I said ruefully with half a smile.

After dinner I sat on the front steps of the ornate church. My breath caught in my throat as I read his message.

Dear Sheila,

Accept the gifts. Enjoy the place. Please not worry. I just decide to go another way today. Only sing a song or do a prayer for my birthday.

Buen Camino,

Helmut

Gandhi gave me his note my first day in Santiago. I had just started exploring the city when I bumped into my playmate, Richard. Without any planning, Richard and I had met in Ledigos and then run into each other in Sahagún, León, and Santiago. Each time, we fell into our unique travel style: Keeping up a constant stream of flirty banter, we would walk around the city, get lost, take goofy snapshots, share a meal, and say goodbye. It was like having dessert and nothing else.

In the main square of Santiago we stopped to take silly photos with what we thought was a white painted Gandhi statue. I assumed it was part of the nearby museum and the coin jar was for contributions. As I dropped a coin in the jar, the statue scared me to death by turning his head and thanking me. He was one of those amazing street artists who holds an immoveable pose for hours. He said Gandhi had a message for me and gave me a fortune-cookie-like slip of paper.

The weak can never forgive. Forgiveness is the attribute of the strong.

Richard got one too but I do not remember what his said.

Later that day we were sitting in the church waiting for mass to begin. Richard got into a squabble with the lady next to him who was crinkling her shopping bag. He said in a loud voice that she was disturbing everyone; she yelled something in Spanish about him being a rude Brit. The commotion drew stares from the priests who were just processing in. I frantically tugged on Richard's sleeve trying to hand him my Gandhi message but he waved it away. Moving aside, I folded the little paper and put it back in my pocket.

* * * *

THE HIKING PANTS I wore on the pilgrimage fit comfortably when I started but halfway through the journey they began to droop precariously. My partial clothesline served as a belt to keep them on. I returned from the Camino fifteen pounds lighter but gradually most of the weight came back. I was dismayed. I felt that regaining the pounds meant losing the treasures I had received. But I couldn't hold that dehydrated, seven-hours-a-day walking weight. Nor could I clutch the experiences of my trip. I could revisit but not stay there.

Research shows that each time we pull out a memory both the circuitry in our brain changes and the memory itself alters. Despite regaining the pounds, I was a different shape. Clothes that used to fit now hung loosely. Regardless of the scale, I was not the same.

The lessons of the Camino were sown rather than learned and I am growing, here and there, depending on what I water. My pockets taught me that I do not need much more than a supply of toilet paper, that time is an illusion, and that, as Gandhi told me, forgiveness is for the strong. Like my hiking pants, I am the same but fit my life differently—a little quicker to say thank you, a bit slower to dismiss the gifts.

7—Second Extraordinary Encounter: 45's

ON MY WAY HOME from the Camino I stopped by my sister and brother-in-law's vacation cottage in the Adirondacks. We were sitting in those sturdy, wooden, appropriately named Adirondack chairs lined up on the front porch overlooking the lake. The water was shimmering silver, rimmed with towering, soldier-like pines; straight ahead a smear of pink announced the start of a glorious sunset. I was talking about my recent trip, careful to sidestep the slightest mention of anything religious. My family was fanatically nonbelieving.

The night before, we had been sitting in their living room after dinner, my sister on the couch to my left and my brother-in-law in the chintz armchair on my right. Back and forth, they were shooting accusations disguised as questions.

"How can you believe in a virgin birth?" said one of them.

"Are you opposed to science as a whole?" volleyed the other.

"Could you possibly be anti-abortion?" swooshed back.

I felt like a ball in a tennis match. Since there were no real questions, there were no possible answers, so I said, "Listen, this is my spiritual practice and I get great nourishment from it." The finality of the statement, plus the entrance of another houseguest, seemed to end it—for the moment.

But now I slipped and mentioned something about my journey including some spiritual highs. My brother-in-law swiveled from the postcard view before us and jumped.

"Were your ... uh ... 'spiritual experiences' all on mountaintops?"

Of course it was not a straightforward question; I knew he was trying to goad me into a defensive outburst. "Heavens no," I replied as my mind flew back to the industrial flats outside Castañares.

* * * *

DRIED PRICKLY WEEDS crunched underfoot while blackened brick factories on either side of the road spewed acrid smoke overhead. The surroundings could not have been less like a mountaintop and I was anything but a serenely pious pilgrim; my usual evening battle was raging full force. *This city is known to fill up quickly so there probably won't be a place and I'll have to keep walking. Look at all the pilgrims passing me by; who knows if there'll be a place at the next town. And this city is known to fill up quickly ...* The obsessive, fear-driven tapes were perseverating like an old phonograph needle stuck on a recording. I couldn't get them to stop.

My head drooped lower as I recoiled from the dismal view inside and out. I felt there was no escape from my misery. I walked alone in the world, alone on this grimy road, alone facing this onslaught of fear.

As I ploughed forward, I became aware of a different sensation trying to penetrate my despondency—like the faint whiff of something delicious wafting through a gloomy house. There seemed to be a presence near me. I dismissed it because I could not let myself hope that I would be visited again like my experience outside Belorado, where the Lord had shown me how I was held like the Eucharist. Yet I definitely felt someone matching my steps. *I probably need more water. The Lord would not give me that much attention. It couldn't be.*

While continuing to trudge on I peeked sideways from under my hat and, thinking I had glimpsed someone, quickly looked down. I thought I saw Him. I began to feel the weight of His step and the warmth of His vibrant company. Looking more carefully, I recognized a young Jesus, tall and strong, with carved, angular Semitic features crinkled in mirth and mischief. Wearing sandals and loose earth-colored clothes, He could easily be mistaken for an ordinary pilgrim but there was no mistaking the power of His Presence.

Jesus looked at me with a playful expression. That mischievous grin, almost naughtiness, on the face of our Lord took it out of the realm of what I would imagine. He was laughing, not exactly *at* me but chuckling indulgently like a mother finding her child scared to go down the slide or stuck on top of the jungle gym.

The Lord teased me, "Your mind is stuck playing a 45 record."

A third grader once asked me, "Did you know there used to be these black plates that played music?" He was shocked when I told him I remembered records, as astounded as when he learned there really had been dinosaurs. Though vinyl has made a comeback, I mention this for those who do not remember that 45's were the small records that played just one song. We could, for example, hear Jerry Lee Lewis belting out *Great Balls of Fire* ad nauseam.

"You are trapped playing the same song over and over," said the Lord.

I nodded and sighed recognizing the truth of that divine description. "You're right."

Jesus cajoled, "I'm going to take that record and toss it away."

He picked up the record, as if taking it from the top of my mental turntable, and hurled it across the unkempt field like a well-flung Frisbee. The vinyl flew in a huge arc across the grey sky and smashed to the ground, shattering into a thousand pieces.

He laughed with abandon.

"Hmmm," I murmured. It was a delightful gesture but I knew this 45 sat on top of hundreds just like it. My obsessive rants were not likely to be eliminated in one grand stroke.

"I don't want to bother You," I whispered, "but do You know there are plenty more stacked there?"

"Yes, don't worry." His voice bubbled with mirth but sounded so very gentle. "I will keep picking them up and hurling them away. However many there are." He bestowed the kindest of smiles.

Then His tone changed slightly, losing its light joviality. It sounded rounded and fuller, more like a pronouncement. "I will stay," He said. "I am with you." The words reverberated around and through me, filling in all the cracks in my being. The Lord would remain no matter how many follies and failings I showed Him.

Then He returned to the teasing banter and we continued side by side. Again and again Jesus lifted out a small plastic record of droning repetitive fear and flung it away. The weedy lots next to the road were littered with vinyl shards.

While I laughed at the silliness of the image I was—very much like on the road to Belorado—shedding tears of gratitude. *Thank You for being so patient ... for accepting me without a hint of scolding ... for understanding my relentless fear.* We weren't discussing my psychological wounds; the Lord was simply throwing them away.

Of course I imagined it all—didn't I? Even so, I wonder where the images came from.

Was He successful? Was I free of the gripping anxiety of not having a place at the end of the day, a place in this world? That day I was. There was an immediate relief with celestial laughter replacing my grim determination. I suspected I would fall back into fear sometime in the future but for now our unexpected, lighthearted playfulness made the miserable flats around me look heavenly. And I could revisit the experience as often as I wished.

* * * *

RELUCTANTLY COMING BACK from my reveries, I found myself sitting on the porch with my sister and brother-in-law. I sighed and shifted in my chair. The memory in my mind was more beautiful than the picturesque lake directly in front of me.

Turning to them, I grinned and said, "No need for mountains."

8—Play

WHERE'S THE INSTRUCTION MANUAL? I haven't a clue what I'm doing and whatever I am doing probably isn't right. Of course how would I recognize what right looks like?

Walking the Camino was a lot like having my first baby.

I remember coming home from the hospital with my infant son; he was wearing a soggy diaper and I was soaked in apprehension. Since I was the youngest in my family and had never babysat, I knew nothing about taking care of him, hadn't even held a baby before being completely in charge of one.

This was the era of cloth diapers, innocent white cotton rectangles held together by enormous safety pins. The deceivingly sweet pink or blue pins were actually lethal weapons ready to poke or tear into that vulnerable flesh. Along with them, seat straps, buckles, temperature testing, neck holding, burping all seemed poised to trip me up and take him down.

Luckily my son was a sturdy, easygoing baby, but I was convinced the world around him crackled with danger and I had been designated his sole protector. I held the overriding belief that whatever happened to this child was completely up to me. There was no family around and I certainly didn't expect my husband to know anything; *Leave It to Beaver* gender roles were solidly in place and my husband was relieved to be off the hook. Taking up the burden, I became grimly conscientious.

About a month into my dour parenting, the principal from the school where I worked came to visit. Almost twenty years my senior, she had four grown kids, a slew of grandbabies, and an aura of staunch unflappability.

"Oh what a sweetie!" She swooped in and twirled him around at what looked like breakneck speed.

"My little man," she cooed, swinging him back and forth like a gigantic up-chucking Tidal Wave ride. If she hadn't been my boss I would have chucked her out.

Opening his gummy mouth, he let out a deep belly laugh. It grieves me to think that, until then, I had never heard him squeal in delight. She blew bubbles, bounced him up and down, and buzzed his stomach. They laughed uproariously.

Plopping the gleeful baby back in my arms, she said. "You know, he doesn't know it's not supposed to take three hours to change a diaper. You might consider lightening up."

So, with determined joviality, I began to play with my infant son. Stupid baby sounds were beyond my reach, but swinging and twirling him became a regular routine. Soon I did not have to force it. Play lifted the crushing weight of getting life right, allowing me to loosen my grip on control without relinquishing responsibilities. I saw that the goal was to do my best while accepting the premise that nothing was ultimately up to me—a foray into a spiritual practice years before I knew enough to seek it.

The lesson would need to be repeated. My school principal had taught me to play with my baby but it was a Benedictine nun who reminded me to play on the Camino.

* * * *

AS SOON AS I stepped onto the trail, I was beset with conflicting mindsets: *Enjoy the moment* or *Keep your eye on the goal.* Sometimes I could grasp both simultaneously, like savoring the vibrant beauty of a field of orange and yellow wildflowers while striding on the path alongside, or feeling caressed by a soft breeze while struggling up a steep hill. But often a choice was required: another mile or call it a day, eat or wait, walk or rest. My nature leaned toward striving for the goal, but if I was going to focus solely on ploughing ahead I might as well have stayed on a treadmill at the gym.

The pilgrims I met seemed to lean toward one stance over the other. At one end was an Austrian woman who told me she headed out every morning at 4:00 AM, pounded out twenty-plus miles, and slept all afternoon.

At the other extreme stood the three women from Baltimore who were intent on "enjoying the process." Sprawled barefoot on a blanket, sharing snacks and stories, they beckoned to me. "Come rest with us. It's too hot to walk now."

Although I enjoyed their company, I joined them only briefly. Staying shod, I chatted for a short while, munched on a few chips, then hoisted my pack and returned to my task of reaching Larrasoaña before the *albergue* filled. They did not make it into the shelter and had to arrange transportation to a hotel. The next morning they got sidetracked visiting a monastery and, later, I heard they abandoned the walk in favor of a sightseeing journey.

How would I find the line between rose-smelling and nose-grinding?

Signing in at Larrasoaña was my second *albergue* experience. My first hostel stay at Roncesvalles had been reminiscent of college dorms, with partitions dividing the bunks into groups and separate bathrooms designated for men and women. Larrasoaña was my wide-eyed initiation into the fully-gender-mixed, at-ease-with-virtual-nudity, one-toilet-for-fifty, twenty-beds-in-a-row arrangement. When I finally fell asleep, I drifted off to grunts, snorts, and farts all around me. When I opened my eyes, I was surrounded by hairy, paunched men all wearing black Speedo-like underwear. Where do I look? Do I avert my eyes or ogle?

I stumbled out of Larrasoaña as burdened and bewildered as I had felt as a new mother. In addition to the weight of my pack, I shouldered relentless pressure: *Get going. You barely made it into this hostel and have to get to the next town before that albergue fills up. No time to stop. Keep focused.* Head bowed and back bent under my yoke, I trudged off as if bound to a chain gang. My pilgrimage stretched grimly before me.

But later that day, rounding the corner of a hillside path, I noticed a sweet, little stone church nestled in a grove of leafy shade trees. Thwarting my mental taskmaster, I veered off-trail into the 13th century church in Zabaldica. It felt like a prison break.

Entering the medieval chapel I was instantly enveloped in cool stillness. Simple wooden benches rested on the worn stone floor; filtered light and incense mingled with soft background music of piped-in Gregorian chants. I sank to my knees and leaned my forehead on the back of the pew in front of me. Ignoring the disciplinarian in my head I sighed, letting myself settle into the quietness.

"Do you want to play the bells?" The lilting voice reverberated throughout the chapel.

Startled to standing, I turned to face a diminutive nun in a mid-length grey habit. She approached me while I scanned her face to see if I had done something wrong. Smiling broadly, she said in Spanish accented English, "You can go up to the bell tower and ring the bells, if you like."

"I can?"

She pointed to a loft in the back of the church.

I left my gear and climbed up the rough wooden ladder, stepping onto a platform containing two enormous antique bells. The bells were hanging within open arched windows overlooking a lush, undulating valley dotted with clusters of red-tiled roofs. Since the church was perched on a little hill, the view from the tower seemed endless. I tapped a fingernail against the greenish brass surface and even that hesitant touch caused a lovely resonance. Grabbing the thick coarse rope dangling from one of the bells, I tugged with abandon. The entire countryside could hear my clanging. It was a moment of unrestrained liberation, with no thought of deadlines or destinations.

The petite nun met me when I descended from the loft and we chatted as I gathered my things. She told me she was a Benedictine, which is a teaching order, but was assigned to this church as a caretaker. When I mentioned I was from California she said she had spent a few years there teaching. It turned out she had worked under the same principal that I now worked for.

"What a coincidence!" I exclaimed.

"Small world," she concurred. "I would like to send her a note. Could you take it back with you? Why don't you come in for tea?"

Stepping into the refectory next door, I found myself in a haven of gleaming, dark, polished wood and white lace. The table was set with a pot of black tea and a pitcher of heavy cream and my eyes widened as she added a plate of fat, freshly made, coconut macaroons.

Sister Marisol and I chatted, our sentences excitedly dovetailing one another as we discovered mutual interests and intersecting travels. We found a shared passion for liturgical dance. With a silent nod, we put away our cups and saucers and pushed all the furniture against the walls. She took off her black oxfords while I pulled off my grey boots and we began to dance. I showed her my choreography to *Hail Mary* and we stretched and turned and twisted in unison as we sang the commonly known prayer full blast. I asked to see her choreography and she demonstrated her folk-dance-like steps. She put on a record and, linking arms to shoulders, we whirled around the room for the entire song. Breathing deeply, we stopped and wiped our brows. Then we pulled the furniture and ourselves back together.

I put my boots back on and as I was ready to leave Sister Marisol directed me to the monastery-turned-*albergue* in the next town, saying she would call Brother Valentino to let him know I was coming. Knowing where I would spend the night lightened my step while the dance, tea, and cookies lightened my heart. But it was the sense of unfettered fun that energized and invigorated me. I completed my day's walk through pastures of red poppies feeling like God had buzzed my stomach and tickled my toes.

And the play continued.

The town of Arre looked like a postcard coming to life. The entrance arced across a waterfall flowing into a river skirting the city. Visitors entered on an ancient rock bridge, complete with moss and tiny pink flowers peeking through crevices, and crossed a rumbling rush of water sending up a fine misty spray. In the central square, children played tag while old ladies sat grouped on benches and a gargoyled water fountain poured cold clean water for the taking.

I approached the massive arched oak doors of the monastery-hostel. The grey stone structure felt cold and forbidding until Brother Valentino, a gnarled elderly monk, greeted me warmly and insisted on carrying my backpack up the twisted stairs. He assigned me a bunk in the women's section and handed me a sun-bleached white sheet. Shyly he pointed out the antiquated but spotless bathroom. I felt like an honored guest.

After setting up my gear I meandered to one of the several restaurants in town. The fish I ordered came melt-in-your-mouth flakey and the staff added some friendly teasing to the ketchup I requested for the French fries. A rugged young man sitting at the next table called out to me with what sounded like a Dutch accent.

"Hi there. Did you vote for Obama?"

"Of course."

Gliding over with a bottle of local wine, my new dinner companion told me he had left his restaurant business, girlfriend, and apartment, determined to walk from Holland to Morocco. I shared the events that led to my pilgrimage and we moved on to talk about his ailing grandmother, reality, sex, and greed.

It was a lovely dinner and I grinned all the way back to the hostel, through teeth brushing, and into my sleeping bag.

Just as quickly the sands shifted.

Throughout the night, the woman in the bunk above me tossed and coughed and rattled the bed. With less than a couple hours of sleep, I got up sandy-eyed and surly. I pinpointed my bunkmate as the cause of my insomnia and exhaustion and hated her.

At the morning prayer service, the monks petitioned for us to love God and our neighbor with all our hearts. Negativity oozed out of me. I assumed she sensed it and hated me back.

"Buen Camino," she said with an engaging smile.

"Buen Camino," I lied.

Thunder burst above the stone walls and lightning flashed directly outside the gate. I had raingear with me but had never tried the pack cover; surreptitiously I peeked at the other pilgrims to figure out how to fasten it. I began sloshing through driving sheets of rain. The wind whipped around me while puddles accumulated along the path. Leaping over one I broke my watchband and grumpily stuffed the watch face in my pocket.

Entering Pamplona I came to a grinding halt. Although I had planned to walk at least ten miles, and this was under four, I could not go on. I was shivering not so much from cold but from fear. I tried to fool myself that the rain had stopped me but the truth was that my old, obsessive fear of not getting a place for the night had paralyzed me to a standstill.

Rain dripped off my hat and pooled around me as I waited for the doors of the *Mary and Joseph Albergue* to open. I was drenched in misery: *I can't do this. I am a failure. At this rate it would take me a half a year to get to Santiago.* While I slumped against the closed door, a thought flashed into my mind like lightning bursting above.

If you align yourself with fear, you throw the door wide for Satan.

Where in the world did that come from? I am certainly not someone who sees a devil behind every bush. It sounded wildly fanatical yet rang completely true. And I knew we were not talking about an elf in red underwear. This demon was an abyss of despair distancing me from people and peace—immediately I pictured my finger-pointing blame toward my bunkmate and my body-cringing dread of the unknown. The pronouncement was a reminder that living required risk. Choosing security-clutching fear would squeeze the life out of me.

The corollary followed: *The antidote to fear is not courage—it's play.*

Play? As in having fun? You've got to be kidding. How can anyone play in the middle of feeling like a wet miserable failure?

The *albergue* opened. I straggled in, claimed a bed, and unfurled my sleeping bag. I was the first one in the showers and found plenty of space on the indoor clotheslines. I was sitting on my bunk, drying out my gear, when a large, beefy fellow entered and chose the bunk above mine. We said our polite hellos. As he got ready to take a shower—climbing up and down the ladder directly next to me—the corners of my mouth twitched in amusement: He was wearing black Speedo underwear. Somehow seeing those ubiquitous drawers loosened something in me and my body started to jiggle trying to tamp down my bubbling mirth. It burst out of me and I sat there, on a bunk in the middle of Spain, howling in laughter. I can't imagine what he thought. The Camino is very accepting.

I was really laughing at myself. Walking five hundred miles across a country with which I shared little affinity and no language, going to the relic site of Saint James who I did not even like, was just plain silly. The best I could do was to take another step and let the play unfold.

9—The Song

I am circling around God, the ancient tower,
and I have been circling for a thousand years,
and I still don't know if I am a falcon, or a storm,
or a great song.

Rainer Maria Rilke, (1875-1926)

ALICIA'S GENTLE VOICE sang us awake at 6:30. Some of us had been up long before, using the one toilet tucked behind a flapping blue plastic tarp and staring at the ruins around us. It looked like we were in the middle of a movie set: The open arched windows and crumbling walls with flowers and grass growing through the cracks looked beautifully fabricated. Our tiny twelve-bed *albergue* was fashioned out of one room of this 13th century monastery started by followers of St. Anthony of Egypt. The Antonine Order, symbolized by a T-shaped cross, was famous for healing the sick through love.

Our *hospitalera*, Alicia, had assigned the beds then cooked spaghetti on a propane burner. Long black hair framed a serenely joyful face and her full, strong body disdained the trend toward skinny sleekness. In her late twenties, Alicia looked both motherly and youthful and her voice rang a rich pure alto. She had sung for us the previous evening after dinner as we gathered in candlelight to watch the rain. There was no electricity here, no amenities except for the fathomless beauty and multilayered history embedded in these stones.

Staring up from my bunk I could see the high domed ceiling and a tip of daylight peeking through the window. Alicia nudged us into the morning with her strumming guitar and simple song. It started with *"Buenos dias, Señor,"* which I knew meant "Good morning, Lord," but I couldn't make out the rest, something about gratitude and service. Each verse ended with "Alleluia."

I stretched and swung myself up to face the day.

As I left the ruins of San Antón's and started the endless rhythm of walking, the opening of that song stuck in my head. *Good morning, Lord* ... I asked myself, given the opportunity, what I would say to God today? Immediately I felt an unwavering thank you for this rich and complex journey through Spain and throughout my life. I knew several people my age who had already died or, like Reed, were on their final descent; no matter how creaky, I felt lucky to be up and walking. Maybe I could frame my thanks into the Spanish ballad I had heard that morning.

It took the entire day. That is one of the most beautiful parts of walking the Camino: There is for some of us the novel experience of ample time. The pilgrimage provided hours of mental freedom to explore memories, follow convoluted pathways of thoughts, and fit words to a tune. Throughout my life people have called me oblivious because I can walk straight past someone I know without seeing them; it is not lack of consideration but a retreat into the maze of my own mind. Now I had unlimited time and it didn't matter if I appeared spaced out.

Maneuvering the words into the song format was like trying to write a haiku. In just a few words I wanted to convey the idea of how hard it was to appreciate what is, rather than request what isn't. I ended up with a simple thank you combined with a plea for help.

Alicia's Song

Buenos dias, Señor, I thank You
Buenos dias, Señor, please help me to
Buenos dias, Señor, I thank You
Buenos dias, Señor, Alleluia

The lyrics were dumb and the dangling preposition grated in my ear, but they encapsulated what I wanted to say: I felt thankful for the gifts of my life but recognized it was hard to maintain gratitude and I needed help to do so.

For the next few days I ruminated on how I only felt appreciative when things went my way. In retrospect many unchosen events turned out to be (corny as it sounds) for the best, like that old country song *Thank God for Unanswered Prayers*. I saw how the loss of a boyfriend brought me to the homeless project, which fostered my interest in the Camino and landed me here; how my bronchial cough caused me to walk at a tortoise pace, which resulted in my hiking alone and opened me to a host of extraordinary encounters. There was no way I could say everything turned out Pollyanna great but it was obvious I did not always know what was best. I could distinguish a divine hand in hindsight; it was difficult to ferret it out in the present.

"Please help me to," I sang, pursing my lips at that incorrect grammar.

* * * *

I THOUGHT THIS ONE stanza expressing thanks was my whole song and I sang it with gusto. Then a second verse made a shy appearance making me blush. I sang it in a whisper.

Buenos dias, Señor, I love You

It seemed so intimate that even by myself I felt embarrassed. And what could I possibly say after that?

The answer came a couple days later when I was walking on empty. I had not studied the guidebook carefully enough so had not noticed that this six-mile section of trail had nothing in it: no houses, stores, cafés, or water fountains. Endless dry fields extended as far as I could see.

Since I had not planned correctly I soon ran out of my three bottles of water. Not scared exactly but uncomfortable and nervous about when this arid stretch would end, I held an empty container in my hand as I kept a sharp lookout for potable water.

A dark-haired couple passed me by. I guessed they were Spanish, probably in their mid-forties.

"Buen Camino," we exchanged and moved on.

I noticed them stopping ahead, having a conversation. They then came back to me and asked, "Do you need water?"

"Yes."

They handed me their bottle—with about an inch of water in it!

"This is all you have?"

"*Si*."

"Thank you so very much. I appreciate it but can't accept that." I breathed in the wonder of their offer and beamed at them. "I'll be fine."

And I was. The dry spell soon ended with the normal sprinkling of villages and fountains. The image of that couple offering me their last drops of water became my heartfelt teacher—all the more poignant by putting me on the receiving end of generosity.

Buenos dias, Señor, I love You
Buenos dias, Señor, teach me to give
Buenos dias, Señor, I love You
Buenos dias, Señor, Alleluia

It seems obvious that love comes down to giving, but it took me days to distill that. Slowly it dawned on me that the difficulty was to give as directed. I wanted to bestow my gifts on worthy causes, preferably those with donor acknowledgements and tax receipts. I did not want my hard earned money going to a bum on the street who would waste it or drink it up. "Teach me to give" was my shorthand request to be open to where the Spirit wanted me to share.

The day I asked to be taught how to give I heard an American twang coming from some young hikers. One of the women in this Texan group was having ankle trouble. I hesitated for a moment then offered her my unused, just-in-case, ankle brace.

She eyed it hungrily. "How do you know you won't need it?"

"I don't. But ... you need it now."

That response was more confident than I felt yet the Camino is like that: Most of us let go of hoarding and gave what we had. Maybe it came from shouldering the weight of our possessions every day. Desperate to eliminate every possible ounce, we constantly reevaluated what was essential; "giving the other cloak" literally gave us a boost. But I believe it was the Camino itself that prompted an open hand. We were in this together—more like an anthill community than a dog-eat-dog corporation. It is this culture of caring that calls pilgrims to return to the trail despite all difficulties.

* * * *

TWO MORE VERSES quickly followed. The third stanza appeared after I had a spiritual tantrum. On the bridge leading into the medieval town of Astorga I thought my camera had broken, destroying all my precious photographs, and that somehow God should have prevented the catastrophe. The crisis necessitated an unexpected stay in Astorga. But that day—that unchosen, unwanted, kicking-and-screaming day—turned out to be one of the highpoints of my journey. In addition to the fun of chocolate and paella, a luxurious massage and delightful juggling show, I met Meg, who was to become a lifelong friend. Plus it turned out my camera was just fine.

Buenos dias, Señor, I trust You
Buenos dias, Señor, strengthen my faith
Buenos dias, Señor, I trust You
Buenos dias, Señor, Alleluia

The word *trust* gave me a hard time. I stuttered on it before finally spitting it out with an internal Heimlich maneuver. I was sorry about shaking my fist toward heaven mostly because I yearn to trust God. Every time I thought I had moved closer to that kind of conviction an unwelcomed event exposed my distrust. *Strengthen my faith* was a no brainer.

The fourth verse came close on its heels. Setting out from the charming spires and cobblestones of Astorga, trudging up the ascent to Rabanal and on to Acebo, it seemed that trusting and accepting God's love were inextricably intertwined. *You love me*, I tried to convince myself, *even when I am unbelievably stupid*. It is a trite lesson, shouted by every soapbox preacher: *God loves you*. That did not make it any less essential or difficult. I knew it was the core reason I was on this absurd walk but I didn't know how many miles it would take to get closer to accepting divine love. I had to add *teach me to get* because *teach me to accept* wouldn't work rhythmically.

Buenos dias, Señor, You love me
Buenos dias, Señor, teach me to get

Buenos dias, Señor, You love me
Buenos dias, Señor, Alleluia

Those four verses took me all the way to O'Cebreiro.

* * * *

PERCHED ON TOP of a mountain, O'Cebreiro offers spectacular 360-degree vistas. The climb to this magical spot is breathtaking but the views even more so. Bright green pastures flowed as far as I could see and red-roofed villages nestled in the undulating folds, as violet mountain ranges stood watch in the distance. Mists encircled the mountaintop, providing a shifting swirl of light and shadows.

Despite the beauty my heart was downcast. For several days I had been sinking into nagging self-criticism centered on being old and ugly. Luckily there were very few mirrors on the pilgrimage but when I ran across one, I could not bear to look without pulling my face into what I assumed would result after a $20,000 facelift.

Lord, let's talk about ugly.

Silence.

Staying in O'Cebreiro, I felt awed by nature's art displays. It was not solely the long range views of endless rolling valleys, but also those close at hand, like little flowers peeking out of the cracks in stone walls, rickety gates entwined with vines dappled by the changing sunlight, gnarled tree trunks gripping moss covered boulders, bright yellow snails. I stood on the edge of a steep cliff breathing in the clean air and unrelenting beauty.

Then the silence broke.

Look beside you. Can you see how that old hinge and the weathered rock add to the overall beauty?

It wasn't a voice exactly but a clear message coming through the fog.

I do see their beauty. They're like part of a Monet or Van Gogh.

Hmmm, mulled the Creator, *hard put to say whether nature or art came first. Well anyways, your wrinkles and age spots and sagging this and that's are also part of a grand design.*
Really? I don't see it.
And that was the fifth and final verse:

Buenos dias, Señor, such beauty
Buenos dias, Señor, teach me to see
Buenos dias, Señor, such beauty
Buenos dias, Señor, Alleluia

As my journey wound to its end I started to appreciate the artistry around me, grasping the beauty of a flowering weed or sunbathing lizard. I began to view the world as a whole in a more gentle, compassionate light.

Along with my outlook my outward appearance changed. Having used bar soap for shampoo and worn a hat every day for six weeks, my medium-length hair resembled a Monet haystack. When I reached Madrid, the last stop on my way home, I randomly chose a beauty parlor and hand-signaled the teenage-looking stylist to do something with the straw on top of my head. She nodded. I was initially horrified to see most of it land on the floor but the end result was a short spiky cut that was, well, cute—especially with my frame fifteen pounds lighter. Most of all, the *Camino Tranquilo*—the peace and openness that comes from a sense that everything is happening at the correct time—shone in my eyes.

When I got home people said I looked twenty years younger. They said I looked beautiful. Occasionally I believed them.

* * * *

MY SIMPLE SONG mapped out the whole journey. Like a measuring line on a doorframe charting a child's growth, each verse held the clear memory of a learned experience. Because it was in song it stayed deeper in my heart.

When my boys were little I would sing to them as part of their bedtime ritual. The song I made up was simple and repetitive, naming all the people who loved them dearly. My sons are grown now and I had not thought about that childhood song in years—until recently. I happened to overhear my son putting his young son to bed and there it was. I heard that little bedtime tune worming its way into another heart. Tears welled as I witnessed it being passed on. That is how I feel about my Camino song: It burrowed into my heart, accompanied me on my journey, and occasionally still nudges me awake with, "Good morning, Lord."

10—Massage

MY GUIDEBOOK LISTED three shelters in the approaching village of Rabanal and—like a faint yank on my sleeve—I felt a quiet, persistent pull to choose the third one at the far end of town. These tugs to choose one thing over another seemed so outside my nature they felt supernatural, yet they concerned such trivial matters I often dismissed them as insignificant. In this case the Confraternity of St. James operated *Albergue Gaucelmo* and I was curious to see how a group of straight-laced Englishmen would run a house. But curiosity by itself would not have compelled me past two perfectly acceptable shelters and risk not getting a bed at all. I couldn't decide if the tug was divine or derived, but I could not pass up the possibility, no matter how small, of following a celestial arrow.

I barely made it in. By the time I reached the last *albergue* only two beds were available and both were top-bunks with no ladders—which meant an awkward climb up the side frame. Given my senior bladder, I couldn't fathom why this place had garnered preference over the others, but I set up my gear and began to wander about.

With bits of moss and climbing roses over the threshold, the hostel looked like a fairytale cottage. My formal but welcoming hosts offered us tea in the garden. Using porcelain cups and polished silver, the British *hospitaleros* laid out a feast of dark-brewed English Breakfast tea, creamy milk, and shortbread biscuits perfect for dunking. While enjoying our meal we could hear the monks singing in the monastery next door, their rich voices reverberating against the stone. We finished up and made our way into the village for dinner, then reconvened at the monastery for evening prayers in Gregorian chant. The stay was heavenly.

Since this shelter turned out so well, I asked one of the *hospitaleros* if he had a recommendation for future hostels. He hesitated a moment, appearing to size me up, then said, "You might enjoy Ruitelán."

The next day was bloody hot. The fierce sun seared through the long sleeves of my camp shirt and thick layer of sun block. Panting from twelve miles on a blistering road, I stumbled into Vega de Valcarce. One more mile to Ruitelán. Valcarce quickly drew me into its charm: sidewalk cafés, shuttered hotels with hand-painted tiles, sun-dried sheets waving on lines, vines and geraniums. It was like a painting of what a Spanish town is supposed to look like. Out of curiosity I tiptoed across the polished wood floor of one hotel to ask the price: 50 Euro ($70) for a night.

As I exited the hotel, I heard, "Hey, Sheila, come join us," and turned to see two women I had encountered on and off throughout the trip.

In the typical hodge-podge of Camino kinships, these women—Dutch, former flight attendants, now married and living in Thailand—had become friends of mine. As they described their lives, their husbands golfed and they lunched. Well coiffed blonds with manicures, they were doing the "Camino lite": Each day a van transported their luggage to a pre-reserved several-starred hotel while they leisurely hiked to their destination. I had met them a number of times and thoroughly enjoyed their light-hearted company.

Now they sat beckoning me from a shaded outdoor table holding large glistening glasses of white wine.

"How nice to see you," I said, as I set down my pack to join them. Feeling like a field hand hobnobbing with the gentry, I pulled off my dusty hat and tried to puff up my matted hair.

"Let us buy you a glass of wine."

My oh my, the temptation. I took a sip from one of their glasses; the ice-cold wine tasted crisp and smooth. It was so pleasant in the shade and my body ached for rest. It looked like an inviting oasis but I knew if I had one glass I would stay and something—the suggestion of the former *hospitalero?*—tugged at me to continue.

"I had planned to go on," I murmured.

"Oh no, no, no. It is lovely here and the hotels are so nice. We'll have a great dinner together. It's too hot to go on. Time to stop and treat yourself."

I was torn in two. My entire body wanted to stay and join them but a part of me was drawn by that quiet call. I recognized that tug: It had led me to the homeless project in the San Francisco Tenderloin, brought me to the Camino, and preferred that third *albergue* in Rabanal. Now it was directing me to Ruitelán. I resented and respected that voice.

"I'll just have water."

I rested a bit then hoisted my pack. Every muscle complained and I felt like an idiot. It was now three o'clock, the hottest part of the day. Not a soul stirred and I was back on the road.

"Eh, *Señora*, it is not the Spanish way," an older man called to me from his porch. "Come sit beside me." He patted the seat next to him on the bench and leered.

"*No, gracias, Señor*," I yelled back and started moving more quickly than I thought possible.

My brain was going even faster: *What did I do? I gave up clean sheets and camaraderie. I could have afforded that hotel for one night; I've saved money for occasional treats. Is it discipline or self-denial? I'm exhausted in body and spirit. This mile feels like ten. Okay, if Ruitelán is not great I am taking a cab back.* And that became my mantra: *If Ruitelán is not great I'm taking a cab back if Ruitelán is not great I am taking a cab ...* Interesting mantra since there was no indication any taxi service existed.

Suddenly a pasture gate swung open and a herd of cows lumbered directly in front of me. An elderly couple swatted and cajoled the beasts down the road. I followed at the end, the final cow, gingerly sidestepping steaming mounds. Up ahead, from the balcony of a dilapidated old farmhouse, a group of pilgrims hooted and cheered. My entry into Ruitelán.

"Take your boots off."

The *hospitalero's* command was stern and unsmiling. His close-cropped hair and steely grey eyes convinced me he was German. With my mind still chasing cabs, I docilely complied and completed the registration process. My host showed me a card with possible services: bed, meals, laundry, massage.

"I'll take everything."

"Take a shower, put your clothes in this basket, and wait here."

Showered and wearing my night t-shirt with my only pair of pants, I returned to the hallway and sat. My still posture belied the battle raging within.

This is so stupid! What do you mean you were pulled here? You think God cares where you stay? It's crazy. It's all your imagination.

Maybe the line between imagination and inspiration is not black and white?

But it makes no sense believing that the God of the universe cares for a speck like you.

Well, if it made sense would it be God? Who said that? St. Augustine?

Cynicism careened and collided with belief as I tried to figure out why I was sitting in this shabby shelter with a harsh host rather than at a lavish dinner in a sparklingly clean hotel. It seemed pure folly chasing a personal God who would take the time and energy from running the heavens to direct me to this out-of-the-way place. I told myself that all this tugging business probably came from psychological wounds or other mental disturbances.

My host returned and directed me into a back room containing a mattress covered by a not-quite-clean sheet. *I guess it's too late for a cab.*

"Take your clothes off."

As I eyed him my mind sprang back to another time I had heard the same command.

* * * *

YEARS AGO my then husband and I traveled to Bali. While he luxuriated by the pool of our plush hotel, I engaged a guide willing to take me to a religious ceremony held only once every ten years. The guide and an ancient wizened driver arrived in a white jeep, both of them wearing flowing white muslin robes sparkling against their mahogany skin. My leader sported fingernails so long they curled in on themselves.

As we roared off, he explained that the nails were from his years as a dancer within the Brahmin class, but that he had estranged himself from his upper-class family by marrying a girl of the lowest caste. Since I had alienated my family by becoming Catholic, we found an immediate bond. He went on to say that the once-a-decade service was closed to Westerners, but that he had a plan to sneak me in.

We drove several miles through a steamy sauna of overhanging big leaf palms and banana trees to reach his mother-in-law's house. Set in a little clearing, her dwelling consisted of a concrete floor, thatched roof, and three cement walls with the fourth side open. Excrement flowed through the front gutter. I knew that my faith journey had been worth my family's disdain and, as I hopped over the river of filth, I hoped he found his marriage as valuable.

In the concrete enclosure I met my guide's wife, her mother, and several family members. None spoke English but they all smiled and bowed. I was led to the center of the room and told, "Take your clothes off." *What have I gotten myself into? Maybe I should have stayed at the hotel.* But there was no turning back so I took off my shorts and t-shirt and stood there in my underwear with my arms outstretched. I towered a head taller than everyone as they ran around me winding strips of batik into a sari-like outfit. Then, giggling at my enormous feet encased in high-tech gym shoes, they fit me into the biggest men's flip-flops available. Handing me a swaddled baby, they assigned me a surrogate husband and we all trooped to the ceremony.

I cooed at the baby and prepared myself for a magnificent event. Since the observance was so infrequent and exclusive I assumed it would transport and feed me with spiritual insight. "Well, Sweetheart," I murmured to my tiny charge, "this is going to be unforgettable."

The temple stood like a tall sandcastle with ornate carvings that looked like they had been poured on. We entered easily and climbed several flights of spiral stone stairs, which was no small feat in my binding sari and borrowed shoes while balancing a good-natured baby on my hip. As we joined the rows of assembled worshipers, I had to hand the baby to my "husband" and use those gigantic flip-flops as kneepads on the concrete.

After the short prayer ritual, everyone gathered around several chalk circles. My eyes widened in anticipation then widened even more in shock. There in the middle of the ring was—can you imagine?—a cockfight! For the remainder of the service men yelled, cheered, and threw money as they watched roosters peck each other to death. I reclaimed my baby and stood aside talking to him, "You and I are at the opposite ends of life yet both of us are still in for surprises." He gave me a toothless grin

We stayed about an hour then my "family" generously invited me to a meal. Though I feared for the cleanliness of the food, I could not risk offending them by refusing the offer. With trepidation I joined them in the hovel and ate some of everything they served. Even with our extremely limited language, we laughed and hugged and connected like a family. As I changed into my shorts and T-shirt, I felt nourished to the full and never felt any ill effects from the meal. Saying goodbye to my baby, I remarked to him, "We never know what will feed us, do we? There is no way to control the Spirit. I sought nourishment in a temple and found it in a hovel. Thank you for helping me, Sweetheart."

Back at the hotel, I found my actual husband had gone to a pricey restaurant and gotten food poisoning.

* * * *

SMILING AT THE FLASH of memories, I refocused on the present: I was standing in my underwear in Ruitelán, Spain, being ordered to lie face down on a mattress. Taking a deep breath, I obeyed—then felt my bra being unhooked. *Uh oh.*

"You will not be the same."

And I wasn't.

What followed can only be described as a transfusion of energy. Luis—it turned out my tyrant was Spanish—took his own breath and poured life into each of my vertebrae. Starting at the back of my neck, he proceeded with infinite patience down every millimeter of my spine. At each step I heard a deep inhalation then felt intense pressure. It was like he channeled a force through his own body and propelled it into mine. Energy surged into me like water filling a dried sponge. By the time he got to my tailbone I was transported and drooling.

He was not done. Unexpectedly I felt a hot rock press into my shoulder at the same time my arm was stretched back like a criminal. I flinched from the pain yet sensed my joints release the tension of carrying the weight of a pack. I breathed into the stretch and relaxed into trust. Layers of burdens lifted off my shoulders as my quiet tears soaked the sheet.

Luis gently re-hooked my bra and rolled me over. He vigorously kneaded my hips and thighs introducing me to muscles that, despite years of dancing, I had never encountered. I gave up thinking and floated in sensation.

"Okay," he said.

I felt marvelous—satiated. If I were a smoker I would have lit one up.

"That was incredible," I stammered. "It was so special."

Carefully refastening my Holy Mother medallion, Luis whispered, "That is because you are so special."

Startled by a compliment from a no-bullshitter like Luis, a blush spread over every part of my newly awakened body. "Thank you."

"Dinner's at 7:00."

The congenial group of pilgrims gathered on the porch, laughing and sharing stories, then filed around a table large enough to seat all twenty of us. Luis and Carlos (partners? brothers? friends? co-workers?) brought forth a groaning board feast: made from scratch chicken noodle soup, salad with fresh picked tomatoes and homemade mozzarella, pasta with meat sauce, roasted chicken with potatoes, chocolate pudding—all with a delicious local red wine. No one had paused to say grace so, before digging in, I took a moment to surreptitiously bless the meal and myself. Looking up I saw Luis staring at me: a little nod and faint smile. I basked in his approval.

Next to me a cardboard handsome Austrian man shoveled in the food. With his mouth half full he mumbled toward me, "You know they advertise having massage. It's too bad none was available."

"Really.'"

While we ate, several pilgrims took photographs of our affable group and the magnificent spread. I tried to take a picture of Luis but he said he was allergic to the flash. I thought he was kidding and pleaded, "I really want a picture of you."

"I want, I want, many things I want."

To this day, when I find myself whining about not getting my way, his voice comes back to me.

That night, snuggled in my sleeping bag, I stretched with sensuous contentment and recalled the day. I had hankered for the luxury of a hotel and the glamour of my high-flying friends. Certainly Valcarce would have been fun but Ruitelán was transformative, like comparing a slick affair with a long-standing marriage. My body felt eased and energized, full of good food and good company. My heart expanded in gratitude while my soul marveled at the grace: I had been nourished far beyond what I could imagine—beyond measure. I tried to dismiss the gift of Ruitelán, but try as I might, I could not explain it except as the caring tug of a compassionate Lord.

The next day when I went to pay my bill, it was 50 Euros.

11—Third Extraordinary Encounter: The Bag

IF THE DOOR WAS OPEN I would usually go in. There was something special about village churches. The simplicity of aged wood and rough stone spoke to me of a grounded faith and a companionable God. When I spotted an unlocked church, I liked to stash my gear at the entrance, tiptoe in and say a quick prayer, then bless myself with holy water and scurry back to the walk.

As I crossed the threshold into the chapel at Belorado my footsteps echoed off the bare grey stone and my skin tingled from the sudden chill. Edging toward the altar I stopped short. Before me was an enormous and ornate gilt altarpiece bursting with carved flowers and filigrees. In the center, the tabernacle was surrounded by elaborately framed paintings of the saints. It was beautiful, in its own way, and certainly imposing but contrasted wildly with the stark simplicity of the rest of the room. Kneeling at the altar rail I tried to pray but kept looking around, puzzled at how a seemingly poor village could afford such a fancy altarpiece.

Hurry up. There's no time to waste here. Just say a fast prayer and move on.

But a banner hanging off to the side caught my eye and drew my attention. It depicted a smiling, welcoming Jesus along with the words *Yo Soy el Camino* (I am The Way). That sent me on a mental tangent of how the Camino pilgrimage, Christ, and the earliest apostles were all known as The Way. These layers of reference neatly fit together with my journey in that I was on the way to follow The Way. My mind meandered down that semantic path as I pictured millions of people walking this path, connected vertically to heaven and historically through time—like a cross—and I was part of that flow ...

I scrunched my eyes shut and lowered my head trying to force out a prayer. *I don't have all day. Let's see ... Thank You, Lord, for all the people You have placed in my life, those who carry me and those I—*

Footsteps resounded through the church. My eyes popped open and my head jerked up—I was diverted by the rhythm of an uneven gait. Glancing up I saw an old woman limping to a back pew and immediately pictured my sister-in-law. My sister-in-law was not old, and until recently she embodied the bustling, take-charge energy of a Dutch flight attendant. But her six-year battle with cancer had taken its toll and the last time we were together her gait was slow and uneven. I remembered her putting a frail hand in mine to maneuver the front stairs and I still carried the sensation of how that emaciated hand felt like a little rabbit's paw. Aghast I realized I had not prayed for her or my brother in days. How could I have forgotten?

Oh, oh, oh, I'm so sorry, Lord. You know I love praying for the people in my life. It's certainly not a chore. What bothers me, actually weighs me down, is the worry I will neglect someone—like I just did.

I expected God to be appalled too but instead of a scolding, I was given a vision of a different Way.

Like a dimmer light slowly brightening, the atmosphere in the church changed. Rays of filtered light coming from the stained glass windows began to glow and the chilly chapel became warmer. From the side banner, the image of Christ's friendly face shifted forward in bold relief. He appeared to be stepping out of the banner. My heart raced in fear and wonder.

Heavens, what is happening? Is this a hallucination?

Before me stood a young, virile Jesus—tall, strong, and handsome with flowing hair and a ready smile poised to break into laughter. I wanted to hide in terror yet felt overwhelmed with awe. He held an enormous bag off His right shoulder, a hobo satchel made out of a brown-print tablecloth folded at the corners. The material instantly reminded me of the kitchen tablecloth from my childhood.

Slowly and gently Jesus set the bag down and opened it. Within were all the people I carry with me, the people I want to pray for: Of course there were my three sons and their wives and my new baby grandson—all busy with their lives. I smiled broadly wanting to hug them. And there was my sister-in-law struggling with her imminent death along with my brother and niece, my sister and her family, and my newly deceased mother.

Then like a computer map widening its lens, the perspective in the bag expanded and I could see all my extended family and friends, dancers, co-workers, neighbors, parishioners, the homeless, my community, my country. I saw those battling sickness and those in celebration, those for whom I care about desperately and those I am attempting to like. I felt surrounded by all the people in my life.

The view expanded again and I saw more acquaintances, distant relatives, and everyone who had crossed my path along the Camino. They all passed before me and were gently included in the bag. However fleeting, no contact was forgotten.

There was the attractive German businesswoman I met over coffee who told me she simply wanted a husband and family. Dressed in a power suit and heels, she said, "I don't want this big job; I just want to be an ordinary housewife."

The waitress who, in a combination of English, Spanish and hand gestures, told me about her financial difficulties. Writing her name on a slip of paper, she asked me to leave it on the altar in Santiago—as did the Moroccan masseuse in Astorga, who handed me a sheet with all the names of her family. Both notes were tucked safely in my waist pack.

The bar owner who helped me with a telephone call asked me to remember him at the cathedral.

The toothless woman selling pilgrim staffs and the farm worker hoeing a field asked for prayers.

The elderly man half-dozing on a bench where I stopped to tie my boot shouted to me, "Eh, *perigrino*, my name is Rodriguez, pray for me."

Each person, each name, was tenderly placed in the bag and enclosed. Jesus carried them all.

Then the Lord tied the bag and hoisted it over His shoulder. With His other hand He beckoned me to join Him. I see myself about four years old, a toddler walking with God. Dressed in a striped shirt and denim overalls I think myself a big girl because I am holding up one corner of this gigantic sack. I stretch both arms high to reach the edge of the bundle and puff out my cheeks in exertion. It reminded me of when my sons were little and I would let them "help" carry a grocery bag that was fully in my control.

I am not carrying these people at all. I am not even carrying myself. And Jesus is indulgent with His little girl. He is actually happy with His precious child. He does not scold me when the cows and red poppies and bright green lizards distract me. He does not call me back to my job when I go off to play with other children. He lets me wander a little away, but never out of sight. Then when my feelings or feet are hurt, when I am tired or disquieted, I take His large, rough, workman's hand and suck my thumb in safety, not even pretending to help carry the bag.

We are told that to have faith we must become like little children but for me it is faith that allows me the possibility of becoming a child.

The image faded—the little girl and the bag were gone. I had no idea how long I had been kneeling but getting up I found my knees stiff and my face wet with tears. I breathed deeply, savoring the care I had been shown, and walked slowly to my gear.

12—Angels and Encouragements

THE BAND INSIDE my hat was stained brown with blood.

It happened at the end of my first week. At that point I had not yet mastered the art of swinging my backpack onto my shoulders, so I had to position the pack high enough to squat in front of it, strap myself in, and tilt to standing. Practical but not pretty.

The morning I left the *Jesus and Mary Albergue* in Pamplona I had gotten up very early—actually I had not slept. The previous evening, I had waited in line to use the one available computer and discovered that my son had passed the bar exam for attorneys. Then I celebrated his victory with a bit too much wine, which left me groggy but sleepless. In the grey light of predawn I gave up on slumber and quietly stuffed my bag to leave. Creeping past rows of snoring pilgrims, I went into the computer alcove to prop my pack on the chair. I crouched in front of it and ... Bam! The chair skittered away, crashed into the back wall, and the pack fell on top of me as I pitched backwards. I hit my head on the metal pedestal wheel and felt blood ooze onto my scalp. Having made enough noise to wake the entire hostel and with blood dripping onto my shirt, I jammed on my hat and headed out.

Don't hoist pack from rolling chair, I later wrote in my journal.

How could anyone finish the Camino? How does anyone survive six weeks of walking when so many things could (and did) go wrong? Stones and roots lay waiting to ensnare unsuspecting feet; bedbugs, bacteria, exhaustion, and heart attacks seemed poised to terminate the trip. The path was dotted with markers of people who had died along the way. It seemed impossible to complete the trek without divine intervention.

Before I left, a priest friend said, "When you are in great need, an angel will appear."

Yeah right, I thought then.

When I finished the walk I could say, *Yes, he was right.*

Looking back, I see so many angels populating my journey it is a wonder I could squeeze by. Some had huge wingspans covering a large part of my trip while others made fluttering cameo appearances.

A Room Waiting

Nora was lounging under a cluster of trees on a grassy embankment shaped like a recliner. Joining her, I asked if she would mind handing me my out-of-reach water bottle.

"Would it be trouble if I asked you?" she responded with a thick Hungarian accent.

I had grown to expect that kind of wisdom on the Camino but not so much from a twenty-year-old. I had met Nora at an *albergue* early on my trip and she continued to weave in and out of my journey.

Nora had a kind of geek look with long dark-blond hair pulled behind her ears and thick horn-rimmed glasses framing her penetrating gaze. She did not chat much but listened intently, punctuating her attention with intermittent "Uh, huh's."

She looked like a studious wallflower. When I had first met her I thought she might need help connecting with people. I assumed she'd be grateful for an introduction to my young gadabout German friend and found the perfect moment in the communal kitchen of our *albergue*. Gunter was filling the room with pungent odors of frying onions, garlic, and mushrooms destined for his hearty pasta; Nora was chopping a carrot for her budget salad; and I was slapping hunks of ham and cheese on a slice of bread for a quick and easy sandwich.

"Nora, I'd like you to meet Gunter."

They nodded at each other without a word and turned back to their meal preparations. Proud of myself for arranging the meeting, I sauntered out of the kitchen with my sandwich. Later I found I could not have been more mistaken.

Because Nora loved to examine vibrant purple flowers or stare at an expansive view, I would often run into her as I plodded the trail. She seemed to combine the wonder of a young child with the resignation of an elder so, one time, I confided my paralyzing fear of not getting a bed at the end of the day. My anxiety surpassed the real possibility of exclusion and bordered on obsession. The Camino had an uncanny ability to hurl us headlong into internal pilgrimages. Many of us discovered we harbored a major fear: Some worried about not finding adequate food while others focused on blisters and blackened toenails. These barely concerned me. I was scared of being left out in the dark and dangerous unknown.

I suspected my gut-clenching terror sprang from memories of fleeing Egypt in the aftermath of World War II. I could still see the border guards ripping my family's belongings in their supposed search for contraband and my heart raced recalling our run to the plane, watching it depart in front of us. We fled to the harbor and boarded a boat without knowing its destination. Landing in Cyprus, we waited for a country to offer sanctuary. As refugees we had no idea where we would end up.

Now at the end of each day I didn't know where I would sleep. I understood there is no comparison between fleeing for your life and seeking a bed, but my stomach didn't know the difference. As I approached my destination village my guts began to churn.

I bumped into Nora as my end-of-the-day distress was taking over and mentioned how frightened I felt.

Her eyes bored into mine as she said, "Always you will have a room waiting for you."

The beauty of that Hungarian syntax: "Always"—first and foremost—"you will have"—no maybes—"a room"—reminiscent of the many rooms foretold in the heavenly mansion—"waiting"—rather than haphazardly found—"for you"—specially and specifically.

Was it true? I had not experienced a lot of parental protectiveness. Could I hope for divine care? If it were possible to will myself into that kind of trust I would have. From time to time I was able to rest on my beliefs but so often I seemed to leak faith; it dribbled out like water from a cracked cup.

The day I plowed through twenty miles to reach Reliegos, I met Nora at the *albergue* and treated us to a simple dinner. We entered a nearby bar where the air hung thick with noise and grease; it was filled with the smell of *papas fritas*, the French fries the French won't touch and the Spanish eat with everything. Locals sat quietly hunched over their beers while visiting pilgrims shouted their trail exploits across multiple tables pushed together. Nora and I edged into a corner.

When I asked how she came to be on the Camino she answered with a question of her own, "Does anyone really know what led them here?" Then she let me peek into her past.

"I complete degree in biochemistry and work high tech—big money job. I was marrying my young—eh, my childhood sweetheart—such interesting word."

"How lovely," I murmured.

"My mother dancing. She see good job, rich boyfriend." Nora clapped her hands demonstrating her mother's glee. "She feel her job done."

She brushed crumbs off her pants. "I love him but felt—how do you say?—like an animal trapped."

"So you got out of it. What did your family say?"

"They thought I am crazy. Then I become a—eh—nanny. I was traveling and they were worried and angry."

"I can understand that," I said.

Nora continued, "In Switzerland I meet a doctor. He want to marry. My parents thought good because he's very rich. But he's older and works all the time. I love him too but I want husband with time for me and—family."

"Well that's quite a journey. You broke up with this doctor and came on the Camino?"

"Yes. My family not happy with me. I write them."

My little wallflower was a man magnet. I found that at the start of the Camino she had been with a wildly attractive Norwegian, then there was an interlude with a hotel owner, and now she was enjoying the company of a German graduate student. What was her secret? Certainly not spandex or cleavage or hiding her intelligence behind eye-batting giggles.

What I saw in this young woman was what I wanted. Nora believed there was always a room waiting for her. She lived the conviction that she was special and cared for, and never wavered from that internal compass. Her authentic self-love, far removed from complacency or narcissism, created a unique wholeness—holiness perhaps—that was not swayed by external pressures.

There is something irresistible about people who are true to themselves—they make those around them more genuine. Nora made me truer to myself and, like so many, I gravitated toward her.

The last time I saw Nora she was snuggled with her current fellow on the bench outside the Benedictine *albergue* in León. Richard and I were just leaving for our city jaunt. I waved; she winked.

Soup

At the end of my play day with Richard I knew I was in trouble. My throat was raw and eyes scratchy—sure signs

I was getting sick. I was convinced the only cure was that Spanish specialty, hot, spicy, garlic soup. Ignoring the charm of León's cobbled streets, I went on a single-minded quest looking for a restaurant that offered it. I found my Holy Grail at an out-of-the-way, steamy storefront café with a menu taped to the window: The first item was garlic soup.

Fairly staggering in I stood at the counter and pointed to the wall-mounted menu. *"Sopa, por favor."*

The waitress responded with a barrage of rapid fire Spanish completely incomprehensible to me. All I could make out was "No, no, no," accompanied by the hand gesture of "Not happening."

Desperate and defeated I turned to the two thuggish looking men lounging at the bar near me. Bandanas over grimy shoulder-length hair, two days worth of beards, hooded eyes, mocking mouths, I chided myself: *Are you crazy? Do you really expect these two hoodlums to help you? They look more likely to rob you.*

With a sigh I asked, "Speak any English?"

They both looked over. The one with darker hair smiled and answered in a lilting Italian accent, *"Si,* I can help you?"

Heavens. When will I ever learn that angels do not necessarily look like cherubs?

I shook my head, trying to regain some balance. In my raspy voice I asked, "Why can't I order the garlic soup?"

My hero began a volatile conversation with the waitress complete with fluttering hand gestures. He then turned to me, "It is part of dinner. Come join us."

That is how I found myself at a greasy spoon in León, sitting across from two gangster-looking fellows. They politely introduced themselves as Nicolas, from Italy, and Stephanopoulos, from Greece.

As I settled in my seat I noticed the boisterous group of four Germans sitting near us at a table littered with beer bottles. I knew them as the aptly named Party Pilgrims who made flickering appearances throughout my journey. Hooting and waving, one shouted, "Hey Sheila, you're going for younger men now?"

Mustering my best Mae West imitation I shot back, "Only because you guys weren't available."

My tablemates blinked at me with mouths ajar. We had misjudged each other.

Nico and Stephan, as they asked to be called, looked to be in their forties, both lanky tall with a slouchy weary look. Nico's dark penetrating eyes darted about and he seemed eager to talk. Stephan's mild green eyes seemed content to be where he was and smile at the conversations around him.

The waitress, displeased that I was getting soup without a dinner, scowled at me as she set huge fragrant bowls of garlic soup before us. Ignoring her disapproval, I breathed in the pungent steam and stirred the thick goop of garlic and vegetables swirling with ropes of scrambled egg. Every part of me felt soothed.

Nicolas began talking as if he had been waiting to release his saga. He took a delicate sip and said, "I work in Switzerland. Good job. Waiter at a ... *bella* restaurant." He mimed smoothing an imaginary lapel and straightening a bow tie; in that small gesture I glimpsed a dashing, elegant figure under the grime. Smiling he said, "That is where I learn my English."

"How lucky for me," I interjected.

"But I lose my job."

Stephan slurped his soup and Nicolas continued, "My girlfriend, she is Italian like me. We go back and forth between Switzerland and Italy—not good plan. She wants to go on the Camino so, when I lose job, I think good I will go, become ... eh ... *peregrino*."

"So that's how you became a pilgrim."

"Yes, I don't have job so I decide to go the Camino with her. I meet Stephanopoulos on the way to Spain." Hearing his name, Stephan grinned at both of us.

"And ..." Nico looked down, hesitating. "I buy ring." Slowly, drawing the words out of his depth, he said, "I see house and child ... children." His eyes were moist and his voice gravelly. "I ask her to marry."

I held my breath, spoon mid-air.

"I propose," Nico whispered, "but ... she say ..." He paused. Our table was encased in stillness amid the hubbub of the room. "She say no."

"Oh no," I moaned, exhaling like a punctured tire.

"I just call now. I ask her to re ... re ... think." He bit his lip and his words came out jagged. "She said she had met someone ... on the Camino. Someone new."

"Oh Nicolas." My eyes were brimming with tears. I flashed on my own sense of betrayal when my boyfriend had found a new love three weeks after our breakup. How deep were the roots so quickly replaced?

"I have no life now: no job, no girl, no ... future."

Touched to my core, I stood, grabbed him, and hugged him tight. "I'm so sorry," I said softly. "I have been there." This tough-looking man clutched me just as tight, leaning into my shoulder for a second. Stephanopoulos and I hugged just for good measure.

"She was clearly not the right woman for you," I assured him. "You'll see. There is so much good in you. You'll find someone who treasures the best part of you." *I hope,* I added to myself.

"I came on the Camino for her but now I walk for me."

We ate our cooling soup, each in our own thoughts yet tightly bound around that wooden table. As the rest of their meal arrived, I thanked them for their offer to share but left to get to bed early. The soup had eased but not eliminated my encroaching illness.

Weeks later Nicolas and I ran into each other at the end of the walk. It was late afternoon on the steep road to the rocky promontory alongside the ocean at Finisterre—the "end of the world." The path curved through a lightly forested hillside with the salty smell of sea in the air. I was heading down the road while he was hiking up with a group of friends, all laughing and carrying bottles of wine. We flew into an embrace. Too old for a son, too young for something else, we had an unlabeled connection. His companions hooted and teased as they continued up the hill.

Nico waved them on and turned to me. He still wore his hair long, caught in a bandana, but the grime was gone and his beard was trimmed. His eyes looked clear and steady.

"Searching for soup?" he joked.

I laughed and said no I was well. Nicolas invited me to join his group for a sunset party.

I declined but asked, "Nico, did you get what you wanted from the walk?"

He touched my shoulder like a blessing. "I am at peace."

Eat Enough

When I shared the garlic soup with Nicolas it made me feel better but I could tell a cold was setting in. A few days later I woke up with a hacking, green-gunk spewing cough and just wanted to go home. I could picture snuggling into clean sheets and lying in bed all day drinking lemon tea with honey. I was aching to be taken care of, yearning for a mom to stroke my head and assure me that everything was going to be okay. I'd never had such a mom but it was a lovely fantasy.

Yet leaving the Camino was not as easy as it sounds. If I truly wanted to terminate the trip, I would have to hunt down a bus or train station, figure out how to get to Madrid from whatever little town I was in, then see if I could change my plane ticket or buy a new one—all with my extremely limited Spanish.

Leaving seemed as overwhelming as staying. The world of the Camino was familiar. The trail, encased in its own bubble, seemed like reality while the off-trail world loomed murky and scary like someone else's dream.

Not to mention that calling it quits would have stung as an unbearable failure. I battled my weariness with the kind of doggedness that had kept me in my marriage for thirty years and teaching for over forty. I strapped on my boots and started walking.

The first café I found that day was located across the street from the Templar Castle in Ponferrada. Built in the early 12th century, the stone fortress embodied the mysteries surrounding the esoteric Knights Templar Order. Imposing grey towers loomed over the white plastic, outdoor table where I sat, and I could easily imagine knights with red crosses across their chests shooting arrows from the turrets.

The restaurant served potent coffee and a specialty homemade cheesecake. Just the guiltless self-permission to have dessert for breakfast made me smile. Taking the first bite I found the dense, tangy cheese filling mouth-gluing rich and the powerful combination of caffeine and sugar was a divine pat on the butt. I shared my cake with a pilgrim dog.

As I bent over, feeding my tail-wagging companion, I noticed hiking boots standing before me. Slowly inching my eyes up the dusty boots, up the well-worn hiking pants and long-sleeved shirt, I came to a smiling face and red hair. It was Philip. I had met this handsome, thirty-something Norwegian a couple of days earlier at the Cowboy Café.

The Cowboy had been a convenient, right-on-the-trail stop, and most of us had learned to eat when the opportunity presented. Despite its name, the Cowboy had no resemblance to the American frontier—it was just grungy. The only food available was what looked like day-old tuna *empanada* (filled pastry) sitting out unrefrigerated with flies buzzing around it. I was anxious to see how someone else fared with that suspect meal and noticed that this young man had already finished one. I asked if I could join him; he appeared delighted with the food and the company.

Between mouthfuls, Philip recounted how his wife had developed agonizing shin splints so he was walking the Camino alone while she traveled by bus. He sighed, saying that this situation symbolized their marriage in that he seemed to always be waiting for her. Yet he had loved her since high school and was clearly devoted. I was an instant fan.

Now he stood near and asked solicitously, "Are you eating enough?" His body towered straight and tall but his words curved around me like an embrace.

The sound of his gentle concern took me completely by surprise. He had touched my deep-seated hunger. My face started to crumple. I wanted to fold into his arms and wail, "It's simply too hard. I don't feel good and can't do it anymore." Tears welled and I leaned down again, petting my canine friend until I could stop the flood. Philip had reversed roles with me: I was usually the caretaker. Having that kind of attention directed at me—even from a rugged fellow—felt maternal and I rested in Philip's kindness like a freshly made bed.

An interesting mother You sent me, I thought looking up.

Philip waited for me to finish my cake. Then he thoughtfully guided me past the towering castle, through the confusing streets of Ponferrada, and on to the fields with a clearly marked path. Checking my pack he asked, "You have water and snacks?" I nodded. Then he added, "Make sure you eat enough."

Orange Juice

That day, with cheesecake bolstering me up and a bronchial cough sucking me down, the trail veered into a steep, darkly forested gorge. The footpath descending into the ravine was studded with treacherous, moss-covered rocks, and the air had that dank woodsy smell of loam mixed with layers of decaying leaves.

When I reached the bottom, panting and wheezing, I bent over, elbows on knees, trying to catch my breath. Swiveling my head, I puzzled over a strange sound. In this eerily silent canyon, there seemed to be a faint whistling coming from a bit farther down the path. Following the sound, I walked a short way then froze. There was a small grassy clearing off to the side and, in the middle, a corpulent man calmly sat at a table. He whistled a tuneless melody while stacking oranges behind a hand painted sign advertising freshly squeezed juice. I stood agape. Like a skyscraper in the middle of a jungle, the image was so disassociated from the surroundings I felt I had fallen into the rabbit hole.

Immediately my cynicism reared its ugly head and indignation took over: *They keep trying to sell us stuff. Will they ever stop trying to make a buck off us pilgrims?* I harrumphed to myself and marched by, still blinking at the bizarreness of it all.

A few minutes later I again stopped in my tracks. Fresh orange juice was exactly what I needed. *I am coughing my guts out and here is a fat angel offering me a big dose of vitamins and I'm worried he's going to make a buck off me? I'm on a sinking ship and rejecting a life preserver because it's too expensive?*

Meekly I went back, took off my pack, and sat in the proffered rickety chair. Like a chastened child I said, "I'll take one."

Carefully, almost tenderly, the man selected two plump oranges and squeezed the juice. Taking a sip, my mouth puckered with the tartness as I felt sweet energy course through my body. Instantly I dismissed whatever outrageous amount he was going to charge for this golden nectar.

When I asked, he responded, "No charge."

My head did the proverbial double take of disbelief.

He continued, "I accept donations but I just want to support the pilgrims."

Gratefully I emptied my pockets, leaving enough Euros for a couple cases of juice. My cynicism mocked: *Was this a perfectly crafted soft sell or a genuine angel? Shut up,* I yelled at my demons, *what difference does it make?*

Cherries

As the days went by my cough subsided and I began to feel better; well-being peeked out like a timid gopher. Then the pain struck. My shoulder throbbed with white-hot poker jabs. *If it's not one thing ...*

I don't remember what town I was in when my shoulder joint started screaming but I picture a long sidewalk on a street lined with trees. I walked slowly stopping every few feet to try a different strap adjustment, or fold another shirt for padding, or shift the contents of my pack—nothing eased the relentless ache. I had long since combed my backpack for any excess weight: Makeup, hair gel, and book were all gone. Everything in the pack was essential as was each joint, muscle, and tendon. It all felt like too much. I was fed up with the trail and myself and the whole stupid adventure.

Looking up I realized that the nearby row of trees provided welcome shade and I took a moment to thank whoever thought to plant them. Then I saw that along with shade, they were cherry trees dangling ripe fruit directly over my head. Focused on my shoulder, I had walked almost a quarter-mile without noticing the treat being offered. Tentatively I reached up. Would someone yell at me? Were they sprayed with poisons? How wary I am of gifts.

Oh! My mouth tingled with the intense taste. The cherries were at their peak. Last week they would have been sour, next week probably mushy. And it was so fun to amble along and pluck the lovely red-orange fruit, to savor the luscious juice then roll the pit in my mouth and spit it out onto the adjacent grass. *That must be how all these trees got here,* I laughed to myself. I felt part of the lineage of pilgrims who had enjoyed the cherries and spit out the seeds.

Up and down the street I saw other hikers gathering bags of the cherries, but I simply ate as I went. Like manna in the desert, I felt certain they wouldn't keep. Forgetting about my shoulder I stretched full length to reach the sun-soaked beauties on higher branches.

When the grove of trees ended I was full and my shoulder was much better.

Cyclists

Are you crazy? You just walked past that hostel because of some woo-woo crystal-swinging feeling that you didn't want to stay there? The next town—what is that?—religious? Reliegos?—is eight miles away. What are you thinking?

That was the relentless, vitriolic self-castigation resounding in my head. I had reached El Burgo Ranero after a reasonable twelve-mile trek but had not felt comfortable there—I hadn't "liked the vibes." That was where my self-scolding took off: *You sound so hippie-dippy. You're not going to live here; you just want to spend one night and now you're getting all sensitive about not "feeling it"? It's eight more miles ...*

It was draining to put up with all the internal yelling, but I had had the miserable experience of trying to stay where I felt uneasy and that was worse than my griping. Earlier when I had attempted to stay in Calzadilla, it had not felt right and I ended up throwing my gear together and fleeing out of there. I knew better, which was why I was tramping on.

Placing my feet on automatic pilot I started thinking how Camino miles were very elastic. There was not much difference between twelve and ten miles, but fifteen miles are much harder than twelve, and eighteen excruciatingly longer than fifteen. This was going to be twenty miles.

I had been walking for hours, a lot of it had been on shin-jarring concrete. Despite the touted millions of tourists, there was not one backpack around as I stopped at a deserted intersection in what looked like a pre-fabricated housing development. *Where in the world am I?* In the distance, maybe a half-mile down a side street of bare, flat asphalt, I could see a group of newly built houses. *Could this be Reliegos?* There was no indication on my map or on the road. Balanced between fear of passing it and dread of adding an unnecessary side trip, I stood there solitary and stumped.

A pilgrim cyclist, easily identified by his high-tech spandex gear, came whizzing by.

"Say do you ..." I yelled mostly to his back.

He was already down the road when he made a U-turn and returned. I was flushed with guilty delight.

Relying heavily on hand-signals, I asked, "Sorry to stop you. Do you know if the town over there is Reliegos?"

In a thick Italian accent he replied, "*Non*, but my buddies they will know."

We waited together and, in a few minutes, two more cyclists showed up. Gorgeous, young—probably in their early thirties—athletic, joyful and carefree, they reminded me of my sons. I felt perfectly safe circling around their map, hat to helmets, discussing the situation. Collectively they decided this was not my destination town and estimated I had four more miles to go. Joking and laughing, they took turns taking photos with me—making me feel like a beloved old pet.

They offered to call me a taxi or at least deliver my backpack to the *albergue*.

It was tempting but I declined. "You know, when I first imagined going on this pilgrimage I pictured occasionally taking buses and hiring vans to haul my backpack. But I have gone several hundred miles carrying my own pack and walking every single step. I can't give it up now."

Hugs, kisses, blessings, and in a whoosh they were off.

The encounter was like a drink of cool water, then in an instant, I faced the dry, empty road again. One mile is easy; at the end of nineteen it's endless. Reliegos was visible a ways ahead and I was quietly weeping from exhaustion. Every step came from mental exertion rather than physical capability. *I will never consider going twenty miles again.*

Another cyclist pulled up alongside me. This one was bareheaded with black hair flopping in his eyes. He wore a faded black t-shirt with a skull and crossbones emblem and rode a bike reminiscent of my fat-tire, girlhood Schwinn. Clearly not a pilgrim, he looked like a surly, don't-give-a-damn teenager.

"Eh, *peregrino*, you are going *albergue*?" he called out.

Why is he asking me? What does he want? Do I have the energy to sprint to the nearest house?

130

"Yes," I called back tentatively. "Do you know where it is?"
"I show."
That sullen-faced kid is guiding me in? Why would he do that for me?
With danger diminished, I decided to face the worst. "Do you know if the *albergue* is full? Is there a sign saying *completo?*"
"I'm sure room is there."
Yeah.
This most unlikely looking angel rode loops in the street as I walked under his direction to the hostel. The village turned out to be a maze of stone streets so I was especially thankful for his help. But as soon as the *albergue* became visible, even though no one was waiting to get in, I left that kind youngster without a word, without a glance, and rushed in to register. There was plenty of room, even a bottom bunk; I signed in and dumped my pack, spread out my mat and unfurled my sleeping bag. Only then did I remember my angel. Scooting out to thank him—hoping beyond hope he would be there so I could offer a coke or some money—I looked up and down the street. He was gone.

I went back in and sat kicking the leg of my bunk for a long time. Pilgrims buzzed about chatting and laughing but seemed to know to leave me alone. *This kid looked like he has been dismissed most of his life, and I have joined all the self-seeking high and mighties who don't even see him. I was so self-absorbed I didn't think twice about him. What am I doing on this faith journey?*

I sat there maybe a half hour, then I saw Nora entering the *albergue*. Heaving myself up I went to ask her if she wanted dinner.

Shepherd

My last day of walking and I wasn't going to make it.
Spain was sizzling in the worst heat wave in centuries and I was fried. Having walked for forty days, I was in a semi-

delirious desert of my own. I thought it was another illness but it turned out to be dehydration. Perversely, a body lacking water can't accept it; I couldn't keep water or much else down. I was one day's walk short of my goal. Even though I had made it this far on my own steam, I would have gladly given up and taken a bus if I could figure out what to do about puking on it.

I started walking. After a mile I was so tired I leaned on a rock and fell asleep still attached to my pack and poles. It seemed only seconds later I felt myself vigorously shaken. Opening my eyes, I peered up at a hulking pilgrim man staring down at me with alarm.

"Oh! I thought you were dead," he growled at me.

"I am."

So many pilgrims have reported harrowing difficulties at the end of their journeys that the finish has been labeled: The Camino Shadow. Somehow we are to pass through a gauntlet before getting to the goal. Knowing that made it no easier. For me it was an extreme lesson in accepting that I could not do the trip alone. "The Lord is my shepherd ..." was all I could remember and I held on to it like a lifeline.

It took ten hours to cover twelve miles, while sipping Spanish 7-Up in minuscule bottles as expensive as champagne. Then I saw it. The sign loomed directly before me: Santiago City Limits.

Heavens. I'm here.

Little did I know that the city limits of Santiago were like the outskirts of, say, Dallas. There were hours of trudging before I would reach the center of town.

A week earlier I had made friends with a red-haired Irish woman about ten years younger than me. Erin and I decided to travel together but because our paces were so different we would choose an *albergue* from the guidebook in the morning and join up at the end of the day. For our meeting in Santiago we had picked a hostel near the cathedral; I had an address and my little guidebook map. The problem was that, as I got into town, the diagram did not match reality. It was the end of the day as I wearily propped myself on a stone wall under a tree and just sat. I had nothing in me.

A man appeared across the street, studying what I assumed was a map of the city. Attractive, late 40's or early 50's, thinning blond hair, neatly dressed in a silky button down shirt, slacks, and beautifully textured leather loafers, he was clearly not a pilgrim.

"Hey there," I called out, "can I borrow your map?" The Camino left no room for shyness.

With feline grace he swung himself on the wall next to me. I was worried he would snag his delicate pants on the worn rocks but he seemed unconcerned.

"I'm Sheila," I said extending my hand.

"How do you do?"

Alessandro was an Italian businessman who traveled to Santiago several times a year. Hedging about his line of work, he mentioned he traveled a lot and was fluent in Italian, Spanish, and English. I refrained from shouting hallelujahs.

We started talking about the Camino and he confided he had always wanted to walk it, or at least part of it, and felt most compelled by the iron cross.

"I heard that's where you leave a rock for all your sins," he said.

"Yes, you bring a rock from home and leave it along with worries, regrets, and prayers."

"I'd have to bring a boulder."

He looked at my guidebook and was equally baffled. Turning to his map he studied it then folded it neatly and tucked it in his shirt pocket.

Alessandro jumped off the wall and said, "Come with me."

"Where?"

"Let's go," he stated. His voice was soft but his narrowed eyes and clamped jaw spoke of someone not used to being questioned.

"You're going to help me find my *albergue*?"

A smile crinkled the corners of his eyes.

I was wary of him, but having no options opened me to overwhelming gratitude for any help. We stopped several times for lengthy hand-waving directions as slightly sinister Alessandro shepherded me through the twisted cobbled streets of Santiago.

As we walked I rambled on about my journey. "And then when I got to the *albergue* and met Erin—you know the Irish woman who I'm meeting here?" Alessandro leaned toward me as if he did not want to miss a word. "Well, she asked if I would go on a six-mile excursion to see an ancient castle and I said 'Why not?' That response has gotten me in a lot of jams."

"You are very brave," he declared.

"Really?" I gaped at him. "I think I've just been foolish."

But Alessandro's comment opened an unconsidered perspective: Maybe I was more than a harebrained old lady. Maybe I was actually brave.

He nodded for me to continue so I went on, "Anyways she asked if I would go see this castle and we did and it was very cool. But when we started back the light began to fade and we lost our way. We ended up tramping through a large pasture and, all of a sudden, there was a huge snorting bull headed toward us."

"Really?" he gasped.

"Yes, a big angry-looking bull. So we started running—I've never ever run so fast—and—oh my gosh—there was a stone wall right in front of us. The bull was gaining. I could hear him right behind me. And we both swung our legs up and hurtled over the wall—"

Alessandro seemed to hold his breath.

"And landed in an ice cold stream."

He roared. I loved hearing him laugh. I chortled with him then started laughing so hard my eyes teared up and my nose started running. He slapped his thigh and I wiped my face. I felt more energized than I had in days.

Alessandro witnessed the completion of my pilgrimage. Had he not accompanied me I would have, eventually, limped into Santiago and met my friend. But this angel was my trumpet herald, a heavenly nod shouting, "Good job!" He labeled the pilgrimage a triumph, making me feel special rather than silly.

Depositing me at my *albergue* Alessandro insisted on taking a picture of me with my walking poles up in a victory stance.

Feeling boundless gratitude I said, "You are my Santiago angel."

"Perhaps you are mine."

13—The Tortoise

*A Hare was once boasting of his great speed and a
Tortoise challenged him to a race. So a course was fixed
and a start was made. The Hare darted out of sight
at once, but soon stopped and, to show his contempt
for the Tortoise, lay down to have a nap. The Tortoise
plodded on and when the Hare awoke from his nap,
he could not run up in time to save the race.*

(Taken from AesopFables.com.)

THE GREEK SLAVE, Aesop, wrote his cautionary tales 2500
years ago. Through all those generations we have continued
to cry wolf, gnash our teeth on sour grapes, and assume that
speed wins the race.

Before going on this pilgrimage I was called "tornado"
for the speed with which I could multitask, stretching every
minute to its fullest. Did you know that in the forty-five
seconds it takes to warm up tea in the microwave it's possible
to peel two carrots? That a doctor's voicemail is usually long
enough to write a lesson plan? I delighted in games like *How
Much Can I Get Done in Four Minutes?* And *Can I Fold Two
Loads of Clothes Before the Pasta Cooks?* I still file my nails
at red lights.

But the Camino will stand you on your head if you let it.

When I began the walk I noticed plenty of people who
looked about my age and physical condition, so I assumed

I would join other pilgrims on the trail. But I couldn't do it. My body simply could not keep up. The one time I rushed my pace to match the stride of an attractive man, every joint rebelled and my unreliable-at-best knee threatened to give up.

I will never again lose myself, I vowed.

Except for an eighty-year-old chain smoker, I was the slowest pilgrim on the trail. Everyone passed me. On a narrow section of path I once had to step aside to let a pregnant woman squeeze by. Another time a man with a bandaged ankle hobbled past, a woman with two children in a stroller and another with arms as skinny as her walking poles waved as they strode off. Beside that, all the poles passed me: high-tech aluminum, wooden sticks, branches with duck tape handholds, even the six-foot tall French hand-carved staff.

I plodded behind. The tornado had turned into a tortoise.

I struggled against my new designation as if it were a moral weakness and tried to whip myself into an acceptable speed: *How are you going to finish at this rate? Those people are older than you. What's wrong with you?* But my body refused to speed up.

To accept my inner pace I had to hurl aside boulders of self-condemnation and competition. When I finally gave up trying to keep up and began to accept my honest gate, I started receiving unexpected gifts.

The first gift to come from my reptilian pace was that I met another tortoise. Thomas and I met in Logroño, banding together to figure out the confusing signs directing us through the city. As we finally emerged from the maze of crowded streets to the open fields beyond, I expected him to take off and was surprised to find him still beside me.

Although Thomas resembled my friend Reed, I thought he looked bland like a bowl of oatmeal. When I discovered he was a cab driver in Berlin I am ashamed to admit I speculated he might be uneducated and possibly anti-Semitic.

That is where I received the gift of the tortoise. Our slow even pace provided the time and leisure to discover one another.

As the path out of Logroño changed from concrete to gravel to dirt, my perceptions drastically changed. I discovered that Thomas was highly educated, with a university degree in philosophy, and I reminded myself that while he spoke English, I spoke no German. In addition, Thomas was a meticulous biblical scholar, a professional jazz musician and church choir soloist. As the scales fell from my eyes, that quiet beige balding man transformed into a handsome dashing knight.

Forgive me, Lord. Please forgive me. I am mortified at my quick and critical judgments. How many assumptions have I made from flimsy outer covers exactly the way I hate being judged. I'm sorry. Thank You for introducing me to Thomas and for opening my eyes.

For mile after slow stepping mile Thomas and I argued, sang, laughed, and rested in comfortable silences. We shared hazelnuts and apples and, on occasion, stopped for steaming cups of tea with milk. I marveled at our common speed and mutual passions, incredulous at the number of diverse interests we shared. Never before had I imagined anyone so similar to me. It left me giddy.

However Thomas differed from me in one significant way: He was a tortoise who did not envy rabbits. It amazed me that he did not feel pressured by competition or worried about getting a place for the night. He leisurely explored everything that came along and luxuriated in an occasional rest with his beloved pipe. He was my live-each-step-as-it-comes teacher and I was his not-too-adept student.

Lounging at a small gazebo a couple of miles outside our destination village of Nájera, Thomas sat on one side puffing contentedly on his pipe. I laid on the other bench, boots and socks off, my bare feet propped against a tree. I relished the rough plank straightening my back and the tree bark massaging my feet. Turning to Thomas, I asked him why he had never married.

"Never found anyone who walked like me."

That said it all. I had spent my entire life trying to walk in step with someone else and had never considered seeking someone who walked like me. As most young women of my generation I was instructed to feign interest in what a beau was attracted to, like a chameleon changing colors to fit his setting: "Go Giants," "Of course I love hamburgers," "Sure, I'd be glad to cook dinner for your friends." When I married, I resigned myself to movies riddled with car chases and Monday nights devoted to watching football. It wasn't that my husband dismissed what I loved as much as I did.

And here was Thomas humming Taize chants, eager to decipher the story of the Pascal Lamb, noticing the patch of iridescent dappled light, listening intently to my interpretation of the Doubting Thomas narrative. *I couldn't learn German and move to Berlin—could I?*

Because Thomas had allotted less time for his pilgrimage than I did, after a couple of days he pushed on to walk into the evening. We said goodbye at a small hostel outside of Burgos. My heart swelled in gratitude for the time together while my eyes welled in tears at our parting. Watching his back gradually disappear down the trail, I thought that if Thomas was the quintessential tortoise, then I was proud to be counted as one.

The second gift I can ascribe to my slow pace was that I finished the pilgrimage. The path was littered with immobile walkers: bleeding blisters, unbendable joints, spasmed muscles, broken bones, heart attacks. Although a generous gift-giver, the Camino could be a harsh taskmaster.

Taking a rest on a breathtakingly steep forested incline, I met a Norwegian fellow who said he had pounded out thirty-four miles his first day, then had to hole up in a village for four days to rest his shin splints. Since he was in pain and doubted he'd be able to complete the journey, I resisted pointing out that he could have walked at a gentle seven-mile-a-day pace.

Sipping a cup of tea in a café I heard talk that just behind me a man had suffered a heart attack. By the time the rescue team negotiated the path, he was dead, leaving his wife to her own walk.

I stayed clear of the young Korean couple who reached their destination village early, got tangled with some unaccustomed Schnapps and woke the entire *albergue* throwing up on a Hungarian woman's backpack. They missed their group's departure and it was not clear whether they would ever resume their walk.

On the train from Santiago to Madrid, at the end of my trip, I sat next to a Brazilian man who had made it to within five miles of Santiago. He had fallen, broken his finger, and been taken to a hospital. Most of his arm was in a splint and he was headed home without having seen the finish line.

Then there was the cautionary tale of Julio and Kiki.

It was a dry dusty stretch. I estimated I was close to completing my twelve miles into Molinaseca and used up my water, pouring half down my throat and half on top of my head. A couple sped by then turned to say hello. They introduced themselves as Julio and Kiki from Barcelona. Julio appeared about my age, balding with a slight stoop and a little paunch; his wife, Kiki, was much younger with pixie hair and a perky almost bird-like sharpness. Since she could easily be mistaken for his daughter I assumed this was a male menopause marriage and tried to shake off the image of my ex-husband with his thirty-something Thai wife.

Julio asked if I was all right.

"Fine as long as the town is not too far," I said. "I used up all my water."

"I check," Julio said as he consulted his GPS. "Three miles more."

"Holy cow, I thought I was much closer."

"I walk with you."

Kiki hurried off as Julio slowed to amble at my pace. With a burst of paternal pride he told me about his son, who was an engineer in Montana. A few years back they had taken a road trip from Montana to New York.

"My son very like me," Julio said with a gleam in his eyes. "We drive, we sing. *Exploramos* towns. Camp in big parks. *Maravillosa.*" His beaming smile and effusive hand gestures suggested a glorious adventure together. As we walked he seemed to glow recalling that marvelous trip.

Suddenly he pulled himself in and said, "I go check Kiki," and took off.

I plodded on and a short while later there were Julio and Kiki relaxing under an umbrella table outside a private home. This kind of set-up was more popular on the second half of the walk: Wanting to take advantage of the pilgrim trade, villagers set out a table or two, stocked an ice chest with water and beer, and opened for business. Often I would say goodbye to faster walkers only to see them resting later on. Usually they would exclaim, "You made it!" unnerving me with the surprise in their voices.

"You made it!" Julio shouted.

I had not intended to stop but Julio and Kiki insisted I join them for a drink. They especially wanted me to try what sounded like a "Carla," which was a mixture of beer and lemonade. I stuck to water but did take a sip of this Spanish specialty from Julio's glass and instantly grimaced, envisioning soapy water flavored with old socks. The couple planned to spend the afternoon enjoying their drinks, then scoot into town for a fabulous dinner of *pulpa* (octopus). We said our goodbyes.

The next morning I bumped into a pale looking Julio. "Ah," he said, "we drank too many and the pulpa not agree with Kiki. *Y bueno*, I go see to rent a car for the day." I wished him well.

Two days later I panted up the nearly vertical incline into the Galician town of O'Cebreiro. I was at a painfully slow tortoise pace as I planted the poles and hoisted myself up for every step. Out of breath and a little lightheaded, I staggered up the final crest into the village and was rewarded with a sensational view of the lush valleys below. Streams crisscrossed the gray and green fields for miles all around. Meanwhile the fog crept across the countryside creating a speckled pattern of sunlight as it started its swirling embrace of the mountain.

As I was marveling at the view I saw Julio approaching.

"You win," his voice arced down in defeat.

I inched toward him still working to regain my breath. "I didn't know we were competing."

"You will make it and I won't," he said shaking his head.

"How come?"

"After pulpa, Kiki, she feel better and go drink with friends. In bed now. She—what you say?—sick as dog. I get car to take home."

He thought for a while. "This Camino is—eh—*importante* to me. I want to do for a long time. Kiki, she is young, she want other things." With a sigh he added, "Maybe next year."

"Safe travels," I said and gave him a hug.

Watching him turn away, I understood that pace was not just speed—it was intent. Julio and Kiki were on two different Caminos. It appeared to me that Julio longed for an inner quest while Kiki was along for the party. I swung my poles in exhilaration for having come this far.

The third outcome of walking slowly was a gift I fought with vehemence. I struggled against it like a cranky, over-tired toddler but it was pressed on me like a long, much-needed rest. My plodding speed forced me to walk alone. Other than Thomas, people would visit my pace but not remain there. That left me by myself for six or seven hours a day.

"Buen Camino," pilgrims waved as they passed by in pairs and groups, chatting and laughing. I wanted to be included. My muscles strained and my neck craned forward but my pack felt like a firm hand holding me back. Ever so slowly I began to look around rather than just forward. I started to embrace the astonishment of a field of red poppies and the freedom to belt out seventeen verses of *We Shall Overcome*. With no companions, I heard birds and wind and streams and was open to meeting strangers, saints, and vibrant green snails. I rested when I needed and moved on without negotiations. The quiet became less an absence and more a well of possibilities.

By the end of the journey I cherished my time alone. Chatter sounded like the static between radio stations. I found myself deliberately hanging back from a group of hikers in order to start my solitary walk sooner. At the close of the day I relished nothing more than joining a raucous group of pilgrims and sharing a local wine, but while walking I craved solitude. "Walking and talking are two very great pleasures," says C.S. Lewis in *Surprised by Joy*, "but it is a mistake to combine them."

Being fully within myself was like coming home.

Best of all—when alone and least expected—I was sometimes gifted with an extraordinary encounter. It was only when I was by myself and not distracted by anyone else that I felt a presence—The Presence—walking with me, filling me, feeding me, leaving me sobbing in gratitude. There was no finer gift.

14—Fourth Extraordinary Encounter: The Crown

IT WAS LIKE WALKING into an Impressionist painting. Morning mist blurred the sky into smudges of lavender, while orange rooftops peeked out from the cleavage of rolling green hills. The road to Lorca curved into the scene and disappeared in the haze. Every pilgrim had loads of road-to-eternity pictures but I didn't think any photograph could capture this artwork.

Rather than revel in the soft beauty around me, my attention was on the ground. Loose stones and deep ruts in the packed dirt forced me to step gingerly to avoid losing my balance or twisting an ankle. However my downward gaze went well beyond caution.

I was whining—a behavior I dislike in others and detest in myself. *Lord, give me my boyfriend back. I hate being old, unnoticed, and unnecessary. The road is too hard alone. It would be easier with him, like having a security blanket. You're able to arrange the impossible.*

Jon and I had rollicked in a terrific romance for two years—then spent several more years going back and forth between breaking up and reconciling. We liked each other and had fun together, but simply could not make it work. While most couples argue over sex and money, our differences centered mostly on faith: In essence, he recoiled from religion and I resented his criticism. In truth we were quite alike in our mixtures of belief and cynicism, but our paths irrevocably diverged in our goals. I wanted to believe in God and he thought that was stupid. We were like magnets with similar poles repelling each other.

Because I wanted to steer clear of his disparagement, whole parts of me had to be closed off and hidden away. My desire to be closer to God, which I thought was the best part of me, felt shameful in his presence.

One time I introduced Jon to my priest and, with his typical Irish hospitality, Father Seamus had been gracious and welcoming. A few days later, apropos of nothing, Seamus had casually said to me, "Don't settle for crumbs."

I glanced at him but chose not to pursue it.

I loved Jon in my besotted way and missed his lush sensuality and bone-dry humor. But what I craved almost equal to his company, was the security of being with someone. I had been married for most of my adult life and this romance had followed soon after my divorce was final. I had not discovered until now that being an older single female made you invisible. From baristas to car salesmen, there was a subtle dismissal that made me feel unsubstantial, like the wisps of mist around me. Being in a relationship with Jon made me feel visible and acceptable. I missed the social ease of using "we" and knowing where I would be on Valentine's Day. He was my illusion of safety, a shred of security blanket I could hold on to.

Give me my boyfriend back!

Looking through the haze, I saw an unidentifiable object in the distance. Squinting at the point where the path extended into the infinite, it appeared something was coming toward me. Like a screen enlarging and unfolding, a life-size image materialized directly in front of me. I gaped and froze with my walking poles mid-air.

* * * *

145

BEFORE ME IS A ROOM in an opulent Renaissance palace. Rich tapestries portraying biblical scenes alternate with long vertical windows filtering beams of golden light. A highly polished oak table stands in the middle of the room with several carved, high-backed chairs around it.

A man, woman, and young girl are in the room. Sullen and sulking, the six-year-old youngster sits on her mother's lap.

"I want it. Give it back to me," the girl whines.

The girl's tear-stained face is turned toward the mother's neck, desperately seeking comfort. Her scrap of blanket has been taken away and she is wailing to have it returned.

"Are you washing it and then going to give it back?" she asks her mom.

"No, Sweetheart, it is time to give it up."

"You mean forever? But I want it," the girl cries. She will not be swayed from her misery.

"There are many more beautiful and important things than that scrap of blanket."

The mother is a queen. Comely and stately, the queen mother is dressed in a forest green gown with a square neckline trimmed in heavy black ribbon. Silken black hair flows down her back and a small, jeweled crown rests easily on her head. Regal but not rigid, the queen embodies serenity. Though not old, the fine lines around her eyes speak of a calm acquainted with both sorrow and joy. The queen mother embraces the child gently on her lap. She is concerned but not troubled by the upset, confident that her daughter's tantrum is temporary. The mother's face radiates care while her dancing eyes gleam with good humor.

"It is time to move on," the queen says matter-of-factly.

Next to the mother and child, the father, and king, stands leaning on the back of their chair. In a rich baritone voice he adds, "We need to get going. There are things to do."

The king matches his queen in elegance, wearing a deep red velvet puffy-sleeved tunic trimmed in the same heavy black ribbon. His crown is smaller than the queen's but is made of thick solid gold. He exudes power and action.

Although he looks kindly toward his daughter, his face shows a trace of exasperation and his voice deepens into a growl, like a lion giving warning.

"It is time to let go."

Another crown sits in the middle of the table. It is shiny and extravagant almost to the point of gaudiness. Diamonds, emeralds, and rubies reflect the deep red and rich green of the king and queen's clothes and the brilliance of the jewels dominates the room.

Trying to get the girl's attention, the queen lightly taps the crown sending out shimmering rays of light.

"This is yours," she says. "You don't need that scrap of blanket. You are royalty. It is time to focus on your courtly future."

"In a few years," the king joins, "you will wear this crown. Now you need to learn the ways of your destiny."

Much like weaning a baby, both parents try to divert the child from her downward focus on a lost scrap of blanket. They hope to change her perspective from immediate security to an enlarged world of princes and principalities. The girl appears torn, wanting to hold on to her misery while at the same time glancing at the dazzling crown.

"Someday you will know your inheritance. You will understand how precious you are," the king concludes.

* * * *

THE VISION VANISHED. The mist had also lifted in the growing heat of the day leaving the hills covered in grassy greens and poppy reds. I found myself leaning on my poles, which had somehow lowered from mid-air to plant themselves in the dirt. Looking around I checked to see if anyone had witnessed my drive-in vision but I was alone. Slightly dazed, I resumed walking.

My mind leapt to C.S. Lewis's Narnia kingdom where the children enter a new world and find that they are royalty. "Once a king or queen of Narnia, always a king or queen," says Lewis. This author—so dear to my heart I named my dog after him—consistently encouraged his characters to view the world on a grander scale, to see themselves as an integral part of a boundless universe. Even though we are mere specks of dust we are made of the same material as stardust.

What does it mean to be royalty? I questioned no one in particular. In the Narnia stories the regal children are heroic, fighting under the banner of the Lion, representing Christ, and battling universal evil. Thinking about life on that scale made my narrow focus on safety seem paltry.

Frowning at my mincing steps and my whining grasp of a broken romance, I imagined putting the extravagant crown on my head and immediately straightened my back and tucked in my tummy. The crown would not be a weight as much as a grounding. If I were royalty I would brush aside an insolent barista or condescending car salesman. I would never hide the truest and bravest parts of myself for someone's approval. I would never settle for crumbs.

This was a different kind of extraordinary encounter, more of a fantasy than a conversation. I knew the vision was directing me to let go of that untenable relationship with Jon, but I also clearly saw that I didn't want to—I was attached to the longing and the misery. The possibility of pulling myself out of the quicksand of the familiar, of being powerful rather than victimized, was daunting.

My gaze lifted. This was my choice to make.

15—Match.Camino

IT WASN'T MY PLAN to walk alone. My friend, Reed, introduced me to the Camino years before the idea became a consideration and, as it grew into a possibility, I assumed we would travel together. When it was clear Reed was not well enough to join me, I asked other friends but they all thought I was crazy. My choice was to go alone or not do it.

In the same way, I did not plan to face the end of my life single. The story wasn't supposed to finish that way. It felt like Cinderella's stepsister had married the prince or Snow White was never rescued. I suspected I wasn't the only one in the world who felt startled at how life had turned out—but that didn't make it any easier.

Some forty years earlier I met the fellow who was to become my husband at a Berkeley party. He was walking in just as I was leaving. It was the late '60's and the house was filled with Indian print bedspreads, tie-dye T-shirts, cheap wine, and pot. He had matted black hair and a disheveled beard, wore a ratty T-shirt with torn jeans well before that was a fashion statement. The hippie life had barely touched me as I skipped through that era in skirts and leggings, long hair pulled back in a ponytail. We eyed each other like a cat and dog and I was pretty sure I disliked him until he grabbed me, kissed me hard, and said, "I'd like to get to know you."

Al had been blessed with magnificent gifts—formidable intelligence, strength, courage—and cursed with gaping wounds—addiction, narcissism, self-indulgence. From a high-school dropout Vietnam vet, he was able to pull himself into law school, open his own practice, and become a hotshot criminal defense attorney. There was no one better to watch your back, if you could count on him being there. We had a volatile courtship and volcanic marriage until three sons and thirty years later the alcohol and ease of Thailand claimed him. He moved there to marry a woman the same age as our oldest son.

When I told my priest I was getting divorced, he said, "It's about time."

"Are priests supposed to say that?" I asked with half a grin.

I was certain I was done with men until, soon after the divorce was final, I fell head-over-heels into a lovely romance. Jon started as my chiropractor and ended readjusting my whole life. I reveled in dancing to the blues under starlight, drinking Scotch out of water bottles at the movies, standing side-by-side chopping vegetables in unison.

Going to confession I chose my words carefully. "I am having ... um ... an awful lot of fun," I hedged.

"Have more fun," my priest said.

"Are priests supposed to say that?" I asked once more.

Two years later the romance was done. The seismic difference that finally cracked us apart was—can you believe it?—Catholicism. A former altar boy, Jon had slammed that door hard behind him—couldn't even listen to *Greensleeves*—and was bewildered and repelled by my involvement and enjoyment of church. He scorned my faith and I resented his criticism. No amount of froth could stop that train wreck.

When it ended, I was devastated but curiously less willing to call it quits on finding a mate. Stepping onto the Camino in the second half of my sixties, I was divorced but not dead to the possibility of romance. I headed to Spain to walk with God, but wasn't averse to the company of a man.

* * * * *

A SPARKLING WHITE BUILDING perched on top of the steep hill. Looking at it put me into the throes of a dilemma: The municipal *albergue* of Villafranca was nondescript but acceptable and available. My guidebook said there was a lovely *albergue* further up but that sunlit mansion certainly didn't look like a hostel. Do I grab a perfectly adequate accommodation or climb an extra half-mile straight up to take a chance on something better?

This albergue is fine. The building up there can't be a hostel; it looks like a resort. And when you get back from that fool's chase, there probably won't be a bed here. My I-won't-get-a-bed anxiety had reared up, but I was toying with the less traveled road of maybe-it-will-work-out.

Muttering how stupid this pursuit was, I trudged up the steep path. Out of breath and panting, I reached the top and found myself in a lush garden with little waterfalls and huge painted pots spilling over with red and purple flowers. I walked toward the enormous white villa under a walkway draped with magenta bougainvilleas and entered through massive wooden doors with carved handles. It looked like a storybook picture of a Moorish palace. I felt absurdly out of place as I tiptoed across the pristine brown tile floor. I approached a thin man in a perfectly tailored black suit who was standing behind a mirror-polished wood counter.

"*Buenos dias, Señor*, is there an *albergue* near here?" I whispered.

"*Si, Señora*, you are here," he answered with a lilting accent.

"What do you mean?"

"This is the *albergue*."

I glanced around the spacious lobby dotted with overstuffed chairs and potted palms. "Really?" I gulped. "Do you have any space?"

"Ah, *si, Señora*. Not too many *peregrinos* make it up here."

It turns out the owner of the hotel had walked the Camino and wanted to support pilgrims so he designated one wing of his four-star resort as a hostel. Smiling, the elegant clerk took my meager ten Euros with no hint of condescension and then walked me to the two dormitories. Each room housed several oak bunk beds resting on polished parquet floors. Across the hall, our designated bathrooms glistened with huge mirrors and ornate gilt fixtures.

"Heavens," I exclaimed, taking in the well-appointed luxury.

"*Señora*, everything is for your pleasure. Please enjoy your stay."

I spent the rest of the day exploring the gardens, savoring a meal at a nearby restaurant, and having drinks with other pilgrims on the vine-covered veranda. Sliding into my sleeping bag that night, I marveled at the glorious day and how I had come so close to passing up this gift.

Suddenly a head appeared upside down from the bunk above mine; grey hair fell straight almost to my pillow. I startled to a half-sit in my bunk.

With a clipped German accent, a man I had not seen before said, "I wish you a very good night."

"Thank you. The same to you."

"My name is Heimo."

"How do you do? My name is Sheila."

The formality of the interchange within the intimacy of the situation made me giggle as I scrunched back into my bag.

In the morning I saw Heimo climb down the back of the bunk. Long, lean, and weathered, with a neat grey beard and sparkling blue eyes, I smiled admiringly. We exchanged pleasantries and went our separate ways.

Hell of a hostel, I thought to myself hoisting my pack.

As I plodded through the morning not finding a café for coffee, I started fantasizing about—among other things—caffeine. Would I get coffee or tea at the next town? Since it was getting quite warm I decided that the perfect pick me up would be a jolt of dark, strong, rich, Spanish chocolate.

Relishing the thought of my future treat, I blinked in surprise seeing Heimo knee deep in the stream by the side of the path.

"Ah, hello there," he called with his precise cadence. "Would you care for some chocolate?"

"Are you serious?" I wondered if I was hallucinating.

"Yes, come join me."

It turned out Heimo had stored three large bars of chocolate in the top of his backpack and the whole stash had melted into a thick syrupy goo. He was in the stream trying to clean up. He reached over to offer me one of the foil wraps and we took turns dipping our fingers in the voluptuous mess and licking them off. Hands and faces streaked, we spoke little and laughed a lot.

Standing next to each other in the flattened grass next to the gurgling stream, Heimo said, "You are warm like the sunshine."

I wasn't quite sure what he meant but it raised my temperature. "Thank you."

Using my all-purpose bandana dipped in the cold stream water, we cleaned up the best we could. I wiped a clump of chocolate off his eyebrow and he swiped at my cheek. High from the caffeine and connection we started walking together.

The trail turned into a deeply rutted dirt road, requiring a lot of exertion to keep from wedging a foot or twisting an ankle. Pushing myself to keep up with his brisk stride, my bubbling, chattering high paid no mind to my squawking joints.

As we approached the next town I wondered if we would continue together.

"Are you staying at the *albergue*?" Heimo asked.

"Yes. Are you?" I envisioned him on the bunk above mine again.

"No, I'm meeting friends in the hotel."

I sighed.

So much for sunshine, I scolded the heavens.

It is like wild flowers in the desert. Relationships bloom and disappear with lightning speed on the Camino. Enjoy your time. It is The Way.

Harrumph, I responded to divine wisdom.

153

Heimo and I said goodbye. I registered at the hostel and fell on my bunk destroyed. Everything hurt: my head, heart, pride, and all my joints. The most worrisome pain was my knee, which was held together by chiropractic band-aids—if it went out, my Camino would be over. Why, why did I push myself to keep up with a man? I knew better than try to be someone I'm not. If the Camino had one lesson to drill into me it was to know myself and stick to what I knew.

Gripping the banister, I limped down the stairs peg legged, putting one foot down then meeting it with the other. Everything looked grim and I was certain it always would. Then I saw Thomas.

* * * * *

FORGETTING MY PAIN, I opened my arms wide and ran to him. I never expected to see Thomas again but there he was, streaming sweat and streaked with dirt. I gave him a big hug. While Heimo touched my senses, Thomas had my heart.

Thomas and I had met a few days earlier in a case of mistaken identity. I was having difficulty following the Camino signs through the bustling town of Logroño: They could appear as small yellow arrows or large billboards or brass clamshells embedded in the sidewalk. One never knew; it was like a scavenger hunt.

Glancing around, I was sure I had glimpsed my friend, Reed. His back was just merging into a crowd of people. With the speed of a wish, I created a scenario: He felt better and decided to walk bits of the trail but he couldn't reach me because I didn't have a phone with me.

I ran swerving through the throng, caught up, and tapped him on the shoulder. "Reed, oh my God! You made it! I'm so glad to see—" He turned around to face me. "Oops ... uh ... sorry," I mumbled.

"Quite alright," the stranger replied with a thick German accent.

I dissolved in disappointment. Until my wish had burst, I had not realized how wrought I was handling this trip by myself, and how much I wanted someone to lean on.

The man I had mistakenly accosted looked at me quizzically. He was wearing a beige plaid shirt and floppy hiking hat, eyes, hair, and clothes blending together in a bland continuum of browns and grays. His looks were definitely similar to Reed's but he appeared rounded and blurred as opposed to Reed's angular stiffness. I apologized again and we exchanged names; then we decided to join forces to uncover the hard-to-spot trail markers. As the city pavement turned into a sidewalk through parkland, and then a dirt path on the open road, we ventured into conversation.

"Are you named for Doubting Thomas, the apostle?" I began.

"Eh, no," he chuckled. "I am actually named for Sir Thomas More."

"A saint then."

We both laughed. Thomas said he had been trained in law, like his namesake, as well as philosophy and literature. It turned out, also like More, he was a devout Catholic and biblical scholar. Having studied the Bible for ten years before converting, I was delighted to argue esoteric issues like pinpointing the moment Doubting Thomas gained his faith.

"He knew when he placed his hands on Christ's wounds, like touching the blood of the Paschal Lamb—" I mused out loud.

"Yes, yes, creating the Passover—" he followed.

"And the last supper—"

"It's all connected."

"One story."

We understood one another so well we could speak in shorthand. Our thoughts chased each other like squirrels up a tree. The Bible touched Thomas in the same way it moved me. Even though there wasn't a lot of physical chemistry, the uncensored sharing of innermost beliefs was very intimate.

Moving the conversation to our own lives, Thomas explained that he had started a taxi service to help his grandfather and, because the money was good, had stuck with it. His grandfather had longed to walk the Camino but had died before achieving his goal.

"I walk for him," Thomas said.

Mile after mile through the rolling countryside we talked almost without breath. Being engrossed in conversation, I have only a few snippets of the scenery, like glimpses through the window of a moving train: a grove of slender light-grey trees like beeches, a densely forested area with a large rotten log on which we rested, a valley of grey, green, and yellow meadows.

Thomas loved jazz and played the saxophone in a band. We both preferred the old standards and blues.

"The thrill is gone ..." I belted out B.B. King.

Thomas responded with a do-wop-te-dum rap of Brubeck's *Take Five;* effortlessly we verged into humming Bach's *Air on G*, flowing into an imitation of Billie Holliday's soulful *Travelin' Light*.

"I know this is crazy," I said, "but Billie Holliday's song kind of reminds me of the second movement of Beethoven's Seventh." Who in the world could understand that?

"Oh, yes, they make me weep."

"Exactly."

Thomas sang in his church choir. In his rich baritone, he intoned a Latin chant that moved me to drop my poles and, in boots and pack, dance in the middle of the trail. The song was *Nada Te Turbe*, which loosely translates: "Do not be troubled, do not feel anxious, with God among us, what is the worry?"

I did not know there was a man on this earth who had so many of the same incongruous passions that I did. It was a startling revelation. It was also surprising to find someone whose pace matched mine. For a long time I expected him to accelerate off but he stayed right beside me.

The Camino is famous for connecting people and crashing conceptions. Before my eyes Thomas transformed from bland to bold and I went from disappointment to delight. As I grew to know him I began to look at my marriage and romance in a new light. Maybe my past relationships were not as much failures as faulty connections.

We walked together that day and the next. Thomas would not be pushed into the Camino race. Even-keeled and disciplined, he held our pace and factored in regular rests. Once—just one mile from our destination village, with herds of pilgrims zooming by—he decided it was time for a break. He spotted an empty wooden gazebo at the far end of a field of tall grass, as odd an apparition as a lemonade stand in New York City. We crossed the field, plunked our gear on the benches and took off our boots. Thomas packed his pipe, lit it, and sighed deeply. I on the other hand, could not let go of the competition.

"We won't get a place. We'll be left out. What will we do?"

Firmly, but not unkindly, Thomas directed, "Stop it."

And I did. In a funny way I leaned on Thomas' soft-spoken strength. He mentored by example, taking things as they came and trusting in an almighty benevolence.

My bare feet up on the back of the bench, I asked, "Thomas, why haven't you married?"

"I never found someone who walked like me."

My breath caught for a millisecond as I pictured living in an apartment in Berlin, learning German, and frying sausages. I exhaled, feeling grateful that our paths simply had crossed.

The following day Thomas left the trail for a sixteen-mile excursion to see a monastery, even though we had seen a jillion monasteries already. We hugged goodbye and I assumed we would not see each other again. Now when I was ruing my idiocy of trying to keep up with Heimo, I was astounded to find Thomas standing before me. The monastery had been closed.

We walked together one more day, singing, arguing, and laughing. Then outside of Burgos we parted ways. He wanted to reach the city that night and I was sticking with my plan to get there the next morning. I knew this time we would not meet again.

(Much later, after I had finished the Camino and gone home, I got a letter from Thomas. He said he had bought a Mercedes Benz for his taxi service, "like the Janis Joplin song," and he included a CD of the chant *Nada Te Turbe*: "... with God among us, what is the worry.")

* * * * *

WHEN THOMAS HAD LEFT ME at the small *albergue* outside of Burgos, I felt heavyhearted. After signing in I ventured into the courtyard out back where I saw a group of pilgrims sitting around a table. Though I did not feel much like chatting, they cajoled me into joining them.

"Another one. Welcome."

"Come join us."

Ordering a glass of wine I sat down and was introduced to Nigel, a formal British professor, and his young companion, Natalie; next to them was Magda, a hardy mom from Sweden, and Hans Jakob, a retired headmaster from Austria. They pulled me into their boisterous circle. It was Natalie's birthday and we took turns ordering wine and beer to celebrate.

Hans Jakob (who was adamant about not shortening his name) and I got into a tipsy debate about whether we create our own reality. I have often ascribed my Jewish heritage for instilling a love of intellectual hairsplitting. But even inebriated it seemed like Hans Jakob—his wiry frame intense almost to vibrating—saw this as an argument he had to win.

"How about suffering?" I asked.

"We create the suffering," he countered, pushing his rimless spectacles up his nose.

"You believe we bring on our own difficulties? You blame the victim?"

He wagged a scolding finger and said sternly, "We choose to bring chaos into the world."

The conversation had gotten too argumentative for me so I just lifted my glass for another toast.

As the afternoon deepened, the sun peeked between navy-edged clouds and shined random spotlights on each of us. The wind picked up and trees outside the *albergue* tossed their heads in wild abandon; but our little world inside the courtyard was still and protected. Our host called us for dinner and we filed into the dining room.

As we were sitting down Hans Jakob turned to me and whispered, "Meet me tomorrow outside the Burgos Cathedral at 6:00 PM." Even though our debate had been a bit contentious I was intrigued by the assignation. My God I had a date in Spain and no make-up.

Burgos was only a few miles away but the anticipated short jaunt took on a life of its own, which included getting lost in an enormous city park and being guided in by a kindly Spanish gentleman. My assigned bed in the *albergue* turned out to be one of the extra bunks stuck out in a bustling hallway, and the exposed position made unpacking, washing, and showering formidable. So I didn't. As grimy as I was, I dropped my pack and took off to explore this historically rich city.

I've always been one to discover my emotions from my actions—like realizing that I'm upset after eating a pound of chocolate—so heading out grimy and disheveled to meet Hans Jakob said it all. I was ambivalent about connecting with him. Hans Jakob was attractive enough but his determination to be right contradicted the prevailing *Camino Tranquilo* and left me jangled.

However, I dutifully kept track of the time and at 6:00 PM went to the front of the cathedral. There he was. We hugged and immediately got into an argument: He thought the sign stating "No Tourists" outside the chapel meant no one from out of town could enter, while I was certain it meant that photo-snapping voyeurs were barred. Magda, from the *albergue* the night before, showed up at that moment and settled it by marching through the doors. We trooped in behind her.

After mass the three of us, bursting with chatter, headed for tapas and wine. Recognizing Burgos as El Cid's birthplace, we drank to all hometown heroes. It would have been a perfect time for Hans Jakob to make a heroic gesture like offering to exchange bunk places with me, but no such gallantry came forth. We all tramped back to the *albergue* but I was dragging my feet.

Facing my hallway bunk led me to take a full sleeping pill on top of the wine, which resulted in my bashing into a door and bloodying my nose. Toilet paper pressed to my face, I scrunched into my sleeping bag and wailed. *Lord, why don't You make things work out? There were so many chances for You to make a happy-ending movie. It isn't that I don't appreciate Your gifts and these relationships (Can I call them relationships?) are wonderful. It's just ... Couldn't You send me a partner? Someone who shares my life long-term?*

Not the kind of prayer where an answer is expected. So imagine my surprise when I heard, not Charlton Heston exactly, but what felt like a real response.

You are not ready for a full relationship.

Really? Why not?

You would make the other person too powerful. You would try to fit yourself around what you think he wants and not grow more into yourself.

Even if this was a chemically induced delusion, I got it. *Thank You.*

* * * * *

HEIMO, THOMAS, HANS JAKOB all crossed my path and disappeared within the first few weeks of the walk. In the third week a demon drove me to Richard.

The icy wind-swept, utterly flat plain stretched before me. I was wearing every piece of clothing I had—two shirts, a thin sweater and light jacket, my sun dress, a down vest topped by full rain gear with the hood cinched tight over my hiking hat. I was still freezing. Stopping for a brief rest I met a couple that knew a mutual friend and we arranged to have dinner in the next town. I prodded myself on with visions of soup and a lit fireplace in a crowded dining room with lots of body heat.

However when I reached Calzadilla I didn't want to stay. I am not normally a "sense the vibes" kind of person but it simply didn't feel right. The problem was I felt bound to those dinner plans, so I put aside my reservations, registered and tried to settle in.

Sitting miserably on my bunk, I watched a spare, sixty-something man come in and set his gear on the bed next to mine.

"How do you do?" he spoke through an extended British nose. "I'm Richard."

"Hi Richard, Sheila. Freezing outside, isn't it?"

He didn't stop to chat. Looking around, almost sniffing the air, he grabbed his pack, called out "Good day," and left.

It was just what I had wanted, but had not allowed myself to do. I took a shower and spread out my sleeping bag, yet still felt uneasy, like something was nipping at me to go. The restless discomfort grew stronger by the minute until it became overwhelming. Suddenly I jumped up, threw my gear together, wrote the dinner couple a note, forfeited the money paid for the *albergue*, and ran out. I wanted to shout for joy. It felt like I had escaped something sinister.

Virtually skipping down the path to the next village, three miles farther, I entered the *albergue* at Ledigos and bumped into Richard sitting with a large group of people.

Richard glanced at me with pursed lips and said, "Did you leave to follow me?"

Even though I was shocked by the arrogance of his question I calmly said, "You showed me what I had wanted to do. " But I looked at him warily.

Among the ten or so people at this new *albergue* was a group of four German men who called themselves The Party Pilgrims—an apt name given their plan to drink their way across Spain. The atmosphere around that table was lively with a palpable sense of relief. It was amazing how many people had planned to stay at the previous town and felt pulled to leave. A young woman said she had been exhausted and furious at her husband when he had refused to stay, but now she, like all of us, felt happy with the choice. Led by the Party Pilgrims we all toasted our escape.

(Throughout the rest of my trip, I listened for any news about Calzadilla, if there had been a murder or sickness. I didn't hear of any calamity but someone did mention a huge outbreak of bedbugs there.)

Happy with my decision, I spent the night in peace and continued my journey. The next day I stood in the registration line in Sahagun, gazing in awe at the magnificent refuge fashioned out of a monastery. The ancient vaulted ceiling was contrasted with an enormous curved polished-wood staircase and the rough-hewn stone walls were set off by grey-tinted glass windows. I was surprised to see Richard two places ahead of me in line. He signed in and waited until I was done.

Looking around he remarked, "Architecture is one of the divine arts."

"Well," I responded, "all art is part divine, don't you think?"

"Possibly music but not dance," Richard said. He did not know he was waving a red cloak to an enraged bull.

I turned to him and said in a loud whisper, "Are you crazy? Dance is the oldest, most universal art form, treasured by all cultures and all ages. Babies dance in the womb."

It was Richard's turn to look startled and slightly bemused. "Well ... I say. Um ..." He paused a moment then said, "There is supposed to be a quite wonderful Baroque church here. Would you like to join forces in finding it?"

"Hmm ... okay."

We dropped the dance debate in favor of exploring this maze-like city. Running up stairs and scurrying through narrow streets, we caught our breath at the marvelous views at every corner. We never found the church but started taking pictures of each other posing in archways or with statues.

"Can you get on that horse with the Conquistador?" I directed.

Richard, who held a very dignified demeanor, made a valiant attempt to mount the horse in the statue but slipped back and ended in a terribly awkward one leg up position.

"Are you alright?" I asked between squeals of laughter

"I'm doing swimmingly."

Then we were off to some side alleys and twisted streets. "Now my dear, stand in that arch." Richard pointed. "Turn this way and show off your ... um ... assets. Brilliant."

Our verbal fencing had turned into cautious flirting. We scampered around the entire city unbowed by the fifteen miles walked earlier that day. At the end of the evening we quietly entered the hostel and tiptoed up the lovely stairway, stopping at the top to hug and say goodnight. I didn't think too much about what the day meant. It was simply unencumbered fun.

But again ... A few days later in the registration line at the Benedictine shelter in León, I saw Richard drop his gear and get into the queue.

"Are you following me?" I chided.

He looked puzzled for a second then laughed.

Picking up where we left off, we immediately started flirting and getting lost in this architectural wonderland. León is a city that combines Roman remains with Renaissance columns then adds a statue of Elvis outside a souvenir shop. Exploring the breathtaking Cathedral, *Pulchra Leonina*, brought out a more serious conflict between Richard and me. My desire was to connect with God and his intention was to detach. It reminded me of the chasm with my old boyfriend and made me sadly weary.

We sidestepped the issue by putting together a picnic: He had a banana, apple, nuts, and dried fruit; I had a stash of bread, cheese, and spiced olives. As we gathered our supplies, I ducked into a shop and picked up a 6 Euro bar of chocolate.

"No chocolate could be worth that price," Richard said.

"We'll see," I replied.

We went to the park across the street from our hostel and claimed a picnic table under a large shade tree. Richard had lived in New York for ten years but his British buttoned-down background surfaced as he brought out a pocketknife to prepare our picnic. With surgical precision he sliced and lined everything up. Then he proceeded to stack various ingredients into little taste ensembles, for example, bread-cheese-banana-walnut or apple-date-olive-hazelnut. I marvel at a mind that could create twenty-some combinations without one repetition. They weren't all delicious but the lunch was a delightful jumble of sensations.

When it was time for chocolate, Richard attempted to meticulously cut the bar.

"Richard," I said, "just pick it up and break it."

With a mischievous grin, he broke the chocolate into jagged chunks and we took big bites, let the sweetness melt in our mouths, and mewed in pleasure. We agreed it was completely worth the money. Lunch over, I was craving a nap sensing I might be coming down with something, while Richard wanted to explore. We picked up the leftovers, hesitated a moment, and said goodbye. I was sorry to separate but being with Richard was like the taste combinations, I enjoyed them but would not choose them for every meal. What I hankered for was something real and hearty—some garlic soup.

Despite getting my soup that evening I still came down with a bronchial cough. As the journey wore on, a heat wave along with dehydration drained any remaining energy so that by the time I finished the walk I was completely empty. The morning after I reached Santiago and feebly ventured out of my *albergue*, I was like a snail peeking out from its shell. And there was Richard having breakfast at an outdoor café. He cocked his head sending a tiny surge of electricity through me; I smiled wanly. I sat next to him and ordered eggs *fritos* and a hardy cup of tea *con leche*. Not having had an appetite for weeks, I was delighted to find it tasted good. I ate everything.

Santiago had been the carrot beckoning us for five hundred miles and now we felt somewhat dazed to find ourselves here. Following our guidebooks Richard and I began a slow rambling exploration, reading the history behind the intricately carved facades. Richard was like an I.V. dripping life and curiosity back into me. When we encountered a statue of Gandhi who turned out to be human, the sculpture startled us into each other's arms. We held that position just a little longer than necessary.

Despite his religious reticence, Richard agreed to attend the pilgrim mass at the cathedral. A huge statue of Saint James greeted us at the front door and as we entered through the massive arches we gasped in awe. The sheer size and opulence around us was much more thrilling than any pictures we had seen. A rope holding an enormous incense purifier hung from the middle of the vaulted ceiling; for almost a thousand years it has swung over the heads of pilgrims in an attempt to dislodge the sour smell of unwashed walkers. I was humbled to be part of an age-old story.

Since we were early for the service we got good seats in the fourth row on the side. A diminutive nun with curly white hair and knee-length black habit started teaching the congregation songs that would be included in the liturgy. My whole body shook as she began intoning *Nada de Turbe* in her pure clear soprano. It was the song Thomas had sung to me and it sent me to my knees. I started sobbing. Overflowing with gratitude, I bowed my head as images and memories fluttered through my mind: Thomas, wildflowers, angels, Jesus' hands, Meg, Gandhi, groups of pilgrims gathered around a table, wine, kindness ... I couldn't stop crying.

Richard put an awkward hand on my shoulder. Then the lady next to him started crinkling her shopping bag and he got distracted. He got into an argument with her and I was left to my undiluted feelings.

After mass, outside the church, I put on my sunglasses to cover my red-rimmed eyes.

"You are ... um ... quite fun to be with," he said, rocking back and forth on his heels. "Splendid time."

"I enjoyed being with you too."

We parted one last time never having exchanged last names.

16—Lenses

DECADES AGO when I had boundless energy and faultless eyesight, I found time in between husband, kids, home, and work, to do counted cross stitch. This intricate form of needlework begins with a blank piece of fabric, countless spools of thread, and a paper pattern of a thousand little squares, each representing the minute intersection of two threads on the material.

A leaf in a floral pattern can have seven different shades of green, requiring a change of color every few stitches. While re-threading the needle for the twentieth time it is overwhelming to focus on the goal. The trick is to enjoy a small section without fretting about how long it took, to sink into the moment while pushing yourself to finish at least one leaf.

The shift in perspective is a lot like wearing bifocals, going from one lens to the other. It was exactly the practice I would need years later, on the Camino.

It is five hundred miles from Roncesvalles to Santiago, plus at least another hundred in side excursions, explorations, wrong turns, and bar hopping. There is no way to accomplish the walk without the goal firmly in sight. On day nineteen, dead tired from trying to sleep with people snoring all around, the last thing you want to do at 6:00 A.M. is lace your boots and walk fifteen miles in the freezing wind/pelting rain/ scorching heat with no coffee in sight. You don't. This is where the goal comes in. *Come on. Fifteen miles out of five hundred is not much. You will never get there if you don't push it.*

But to focus solely on the goal loses the walk. Tunnel vision set on getting there—even if "there" is dinner at the end of the day—will make you miserable. Each step will be a burden holding you back from what you want. The lens has to draw in from distant to immediate: *That rain feels soft on my face and those navy-blue clouds look like something out of a Renaissance painting. My pack is snug and this stretch of trail is paved. I don't need to scurry out of the rain; it's quite lovely.*

Every day, maybe thousands of times a day, the lenses go back and forth—until you forget you are wearing glasses.

* * * *

FINISHING THE CAMINO is like finding the end of a rainbow. Where exactly is it? At the Santiago City Limits sign? On the steps of the cathedral? Or when you get home and unpack? There is the expectation that everything will be different when it's done. Like any accomplishment that changes us—landing the job, getting married, buying a house—we are different but recognizable; we have taken ourselves along. What changes is the lens of how we view ourselves.

"Hi there," the man at the adjacent table greeted me. "Did you vote for Obama?"

"Of course." I smiled at him.

We were sitting outside at a café in the town of Arre. The nun at Zabaldica had suggested I stay here and it was easy to see why. The ancient stone monastery-*albergue* spoke of a quiet, pervasive spirituality and the village as a whole had a storybook charm.

"Why do you ask?" I looked over at his table quizzically, while munching on a French fry.

"Says a lot," he responded.

Introducing himself, Eric brought his plate and bottle of wine to my table. He looked to be in his forties with chiseled features and an animal grace. Years ago I would have been intimidated by his stunning good looks; I would have self-consciously searched for what to say while trying to quiet my blazing red cheeks. But one of the freedoms—and losses—of old age is that no one thinks you are hitting on them. Lately, if visible at all, it felt like people saw me as a sweet old grandma, akin to a squishy cinnamon bun.

My new tablemate told me he had owned a restaurant in Amsterdam, had built it from scratch into a thriving hotspot in the city. "It was fun, all that drinking and money and women."

"I bet."

"Yes. Yes ... I'll miss it. But it began to own me. You know I felt—what?—trapped by all that *fun* every night. The days and nights started to feel all the same."

Picturing my sons and their propensity for partying I said, "I can think of people who would love that kind of repetition."

"Well, twelve years ... I ... I didn't *want* anything anymore. So I decided to leave it all. I sold the restaurant and gave up my apartment, said goodbye to my girlfriend and family. The hardest goodbye was to my grandmother because I might not see her again." He took a long draw from his wine as if it were a beer. "I started walking from my front door in Amsterdam."

"Wow," I exclaimed.

"I'm walking to Morocco."

"Wow."

I wondered if I reminded him of his grandmother. It was lovely that he felt free to open up with me. But deep inside—if I were honest—I didn't like it. I felt about his age, trapped in a bun costume.

Just then a cute, twenty-something came flitting by in barely-there shorts and a tank top. Her movements were bird-like quick and she kept flicking her hair back. Her eyes locked on Eric. "Buen Camino there," she drawled as she moved sideways toward him. "Didn't I see you on the trail earlier?"

"Uh ... yes ... hello."

Folding my arms across my chest, I sat back to watch.

Her voice got smaller, higher, and faster. "You sure'd be welcome to join us." Pointing to a table on the other side of the patio, she bent a little closer. "Over there." Was she actually batting her eyes? She lifted her hand and waved, vibrating it side to side, then flew away.

Dear God are we women so obvious? Did I ever look like that? I don't think so. But I miss the dance and the excitement of possibilities.

"I want to be different," Eric said somberly. "I want to be more than this."

We ate our meal and I noticed him glancing at the girl now and then; when I peeked over, I saw that she studiously avoided looking at him. Finishing up, we hugged and wished each other well. I smiled seeing him saunter to her table.

Well so much for different, I thought as I sat sipping the last dregs of my wine. Yet I wanted to be different too. I didn't want to reach the end of my life still hoping to change, still striving to accept (and not rail against) things like the second toe on my right foot that was twisting because of a growing bunion and which prevented me from wearing heels. I wanted to be grateful for being able to put on my boots and walk this far.

The lens projecting my old age made me cringe. But if I could pull it back, I would see today—and this day had been lovely.

* * * *

WHEN I GOT TO the *albergue* in Santo Domingo I found something marvelous: a washing machine. If I washed all my clothes, I would only have my raingear to wear while waiting for them to dry. Since the day was cool and overcast I decided this was the perfect opportunity. I washed every single thing I had and stood in the shower with my rain pants and jacket ready for me.

My thoughts drifted to my middle son who loves showers and often takes two a day. A month before I left for Spain he had called and said he wanted to come with me.

I was flabbergasted by his suggestion. "Are you kidding?"

"No, it sounds ... interesting."

I knew that was utter BS. That boy was so fastidious he would have hated this pilgrimage. The walking would have been tolerable but the hostels with communal everything would have made him gag. What was going on?

"What's going on?" I asked.

"Uh ... I just thought I would keep you company." He trailed off.

Oh. He was worried about me. My heart squeezed in tenderness for him. He wasn't sure I could make it on my own and was willing to put himself through torture to make sure I was safe.

When had the parent-child roles reversed? One day I was helping him carry his diorama to school, then teaching him to drive and then ... When did my kids become bigger and stronger than me? My son's attempt at protecting me filled me with gratitude, yet at the same time it deflated me. If he saw me as frail and powerless maybe it was true—or soon would be. In the future would I depend on my sons more, handing over my checkbook and asking their advice for every decision? Would my only excitement come from watching their lives unfold? *Over my dead body* I prayed.

"Honey, we both know you would hate it. I thank you so very much but I think I can handle this myself. I love you."

Stepping out of the shower, I used my nonabsorbent, microfiber towel and put my raingear on. I went outside the *albergue* to look around Santo Domingo. Hearing an American accent from the man sitting at a plastic table across the street, I stopped to say hello. We introduced ourselves and Marty looked at me warily.

"Is that what you wear hiking?"

"Oh no." I blushed. "All my clothes are on the line. Gortex was the only thing left."

He laughed with me.

Fit, fiftyish and fair-haired, he was quite attractive with a wide-eyed gaze that seemed to focus solely on me. *Lord I miss the game. He is at least ten years younger than me and I would feel foolish trying to flirt. I could never let him think I was interested; he might see me like that garish grandmother in the cartoons. Better play it old and safe.*

"What do you do when you're not walking?" I asked.

"I pastor a large church in Washington," Marty began. "I love my work but I seem to be constantly caretaking." I thought I heard a bit of pulpit resonance in his voice.

"That's a role we mothers are familiar with."

"Well, we have over two thousand members. I accompany them through their major life transitions—births, marriages, deaths—and do pastoral counseling too."

The late afternoon sun started to break through the clouds and my raingear, which had been comfortable at the start of the day, trapped every bit of rising body heat. I began to perspire, sweat trickling through my hair and down my neck. My attention alternated between my increasing discomfort and my growing interest in Marty's story.

"Hmmm. That's a lot of life journeys," I said.

Marty was warming to the subject. "Yes, I love it, I really do. But that was why I wanted to walk the Camino by myself. I didn't plan for other people to join me, but my sister and son decided to come. I'm waiting for them now."

I wiped my face and neck. Not wearing any underwear I couldn't open the jacket. I took a long drink from my water bottle feeling as if I were in a sauna. My mind kept picturing the clothes I had on the line and my growing discomfort narrowed any attention outside myself into a very small aperture.

"I'm worried about them," Marty said, bringing me back to our conversation. "My sister isn't in very good shape and my son is ... uh ... distracted. I'm not sure if I should walk back to find them or just wait."

Jumping up, I called, "Be right back," and ran into the *albergue*.

Ten minutes later I returned wearing soggy clothes. Marty was not at the table but there was a round woman with a bright red face and short, dust-matted hair. She had her feet up on another chair. I asked if she was Marty's sister.

"Yay-yes, I'm Sasha," she answered with an underlying drawl. Her breath sounded uneven and labored, "Marty went to check if there was ice for my knees."

"You had a rough trek in?"

"Yay-yes. Don't tell my brother I had to take a cab for most of the way. But I want to show him I can do it."

It was so typical of Camino conversations to jump into the heart of matters. Marty's return saved me from asking Sasha why she felt she had to prove herself to her brother.

"They didn't have ice," he said, "so I got you a cold soda can to put on your knees."

I decided it was a good time for wine. Going into the dim bar I could feel the taken-off-the-line-too-soon clothes stick to me, sending a chill. My skin recalled that same sensation from when I was a young girl. When we came to the States from Egypt my mother had never done housework and she found it overwhelming. Often our clothes came straight out of the washing machine with a quick iron to dry them a little. I remembered so clearly leaving for school in damp clothes and how they made me shiver.

Hopefully my mother was at peace now because throughout her life she never stopped railing at fate for shoving her out of her luxurious house in Egypt and dumping her in a middle-class suburb of Chicago. She never made peace with where she was.

Lord, will I ever accept where I am? I keep going back and forth between trying to look attractive and feeling too old to be desirable. The age lens never settles.

I ordered a bottle of local red with three glasses and when I got back outside, a gangly teenage boy about sixteen years old was draped over a chair at the table. Marty introduced his son Jason and I was surprised to receive a formal handshake.

"Yeah," Jason continued, "I met this cool group from Sweden and they're staying at the *albergue* on the other side of town. I'll just meet you in ..." He looked at the guidebook. "at Bel-o-rado tomorrow."

"How about some pizza before you go?" I heard Marty's caretaking concern.

"Sure. And some beer with it?" Jason asked with eyebrows raised innocently. Marty glanced at me as he ordered the pizza and beer for his underage son and I smiled, relaying my understanding of his indulgence.

My clothes were drying unevenly and I could feel the last moist patches disappear.

Two German college students joined us, both had long hair, one straight down his back and the other in a ponytail.

"*Ja*, we take the summer off to walk," one started.

"No need to start big business job," the other continued.

"We don't so much like the racing rats." They both grinned.

Their endearing naïveté, believing they were unique by sporting long hair and putting off career choices, made me laugh.

A small wiry woman from Australia pulled up a chair and began recounting her breakneck speed for the last twenty-five miles.

"Yes, I am well under four miles an hour now," she said. "I think I can beat the guidebook and finish the trip in four weeks."

Lord, Lord, how much of our lives do we actually live? It seems like we spend our time—Your time—the spacious yet minuscule time we have—the precious time You give us— viewing this life through a very small lens.

We pulled out apples and nuts and granola bars to share with the pizza, beer, and wine. There was a lot of laughter with gesturing hand movements and overlapping stories. I sat back and smiled but did not say much. It was so clear that each of us views the world through our own lenses and I wondered what it would be like to take the glasses off.

17—Dave

I LET OUT A WEARY SIGH and sank to my knees. Hooking my right foot under the kneeler I rested my butt on the pew behind me, keeping weight off that barely held together right knee. Even though I had walked only a few miles that day, I was bone tired. This was the middle of the journey, without the adrenaline of the beginning or what I hoped would be the exhilaration of the end. And the daily routine had become humdrum: walk, find an *albergue*, shower, wash one shirt and put on the other, connect with pilgrims and have dinner, hope for sleep, repeat. I was bored of walking and with myself.

Surprised to see the church open, I noticed several people scattered inside, but did not give it much mind. I was determined to feel miserable and wanted to plunge into desolate prayer.

Lord, I feel like everything is up to me and I'm tired of fighting. It seems a constant battle keeping discouragement and loneliness at bay. Would You consider sending me a man? Someone to walk with me in this life? A partner would make everything lighter. I know, I know, I know I have so many blessings but ...

I felt his presence before any other senses got engaged. The cool, cavernous room had suddenly filled with warmth. Then the other side of my kneeler squeaked and sunk down. My eyes were closed with my forehead resting on clenched fists; slowly I pivoted my head and half opened my eyes to take a peek. There, at the end of the kneeler, was the biggest man I had ever seen—he looked like a truck. His skin was luminescent ebony, with an almost blue sheen and he countered my surreptitious glance with a gleaming smile.

I jerked my head back to prayer position: *Lord that was not the man I had in mind.*

A chime announced the beginning of mass. Now I understood why the church was open and peopled. I had not encountered a mid-week morning service on the trail and was glad to have stumbled in at the right time. We all stood as the priest and two altar boys entered.

During the opening prayers I noticed more of my pew mate. Very worn grey sneakers and enormous faded cargo shorts, he wasn't fat but tall and wide, taking up the entire rest of the pew. I would have placed him at about thirty years old but it was impossible to tell from that expansive face. Clearly he was a pilgrim with his backpack and hat but the pack, held together with rope, was so very small. I thought my pack was pared down to the bone but he was traveling with nothing.

What struck me most forcefully was the scent: I expected the usual sour, dried sweat smell of an unwashed pilgrim but instead he exuded an earthy fragrance like when I'd dug into rich fertile soil to plant my vegetable garden. Then there was his voice. The opening song was one of my favorites, *Resucitó*, and he sang the hip-swinging Latin rhythm in a full resonant baritone; my voice sounded puny and thin in comparison.

The service continued but, not understanding much Spanish, I got tired of picking out words and went back to internally whining about how alone I felt. Standing for The Lord's Prayer, I automatically extended my arms for the usual handholding and felt my hand enveloped in a bear paw; my normally sturdy fingers felt small and delicate within his giant callused hand. "Peace be with you," we said and barely hugged.

As the priest exited, I nodded goodbye then hoisted my pack and headed out.

Catching up to me, he said, "Hi, I'm Dave."

No, no, no Lord I don't want to walk with this poor, strange man and exchange stories and try to feign interest. I just wanted to wallow in longing and what-could-have-been.

"Hi," I said sighing in resignation, "can't quite place your accent."

"I'm originally from Nicaragua but I've lived in the States for twelve years." He smiled. The contrast of his strong white teeth against the deep blackness of his skin made his smile even brighter.

"Oh, what part of the States?" I asked, not really caring.

"Mostly Los Angeles but different places."

"How come you moved so much?"

"Eh, seeing the country, looking for work." Dave turned and looked fully at me. His eyes were gentle yet penetrating: "You're walking alone." It was more a statement than a question.

Bam! My thoughts exploded. *There it is: He's a scammer. He's going to hit me up for something, probably money. Or maybe he's a serial killer looking for his next victim ...* I knew that was crazy. Dave exuded kindness, charging the atmosphere with his warm, vibrant presence. What really made me squirm was that he saw me. He had pierced my aloof armor and reached my core. *Yes I'm walking alone. A thirty-year marriage and promising romance both behind me. I have failed and I'm walking totally alone.*

"Yes," I answered.

We started walking on an open dirt trail in a lightly forested area. Dappled light made leaf-like patterns on the ground and across our faces.

A bit more intrigued, I asked, "How did you get here?"

Dave unleashed a story that grabbed me and ate up the miles. "My mother couldn't take the beatings anymore so she left ... went to L.A. ... left my brother and me along with our father."

"I'm so sorry. How old were you?"

"Four. My brother was seven. We went to live with my older stepbrother and his wife. We found he was a mean drunk too. My brother just started roaming the streets, but I would wait in the bushes outside the window until he passed out." We walked in silence for a bit then Dave continued, "My sister-in-law snuck food out to me. I loved her very much."

"Oh good heavens. What happened to her?"

"She died."

My shoulders sagged with the extra weight of sorrow. "I'm so sorry."

After a pause Dave added, "That was when I hitched to L.A."

"By yourself?" Dave nodded yes. I sighed and muttered, "How does God allow such things?"

Birds and wind whispered nearby. We were quiet in our own thoughts with just the sound of our padding steps.

Then Dave said, "I don't know about God *allowing* these things. There is free—"

"Oh that's bull," I snapped, whirling around to face him. Gruesome pictures flitted through my mind: children with distended bellies, hollow-eyed mothers, young girls pleading with abductors. I lashed out, "If God could intervene and didn't, isn't that *allow*?" My outburst circled around us and flew off.

Quietly Dave asked, "How do you know he didn't?"

"Didn't what?"

"Intervene."

"At four years old you were hiding in the bushes to avoid being beaten and your sister-in-law had to sneak food to you—"

"She showed me love," Dave said. "She was very kind. And an uncle took me to the construction sites he was working on; he trained me to build, do electrical, all that. He taught me to read."

"You're saying that the love they showed was God?"

"Wasn't it?"

"What about the suffering?" I asked the age-old question.

Dave's voice and eyes softened even more, "I believe ... I know God suffered with me. I felt the love and warmth around me."

This man had been dealt a terrible hand yet was full of joyous gratitude. I felt small next to him. But it wasn't Dave who had diminished me. He seemed delighted to be walking next to me and he was the one who dwarfed his pace to match mine. He never showed impatience to stride ahead.

"What about your brother wandering the streets?"

"He chose to join a gang. I haven't talked to him in many years."

The wind kicked up blustery gusts and clouds closed in. Weather was an intimate companion on the walk. I consistently monitored the heat and observed the clouds for possible threats of rain. It was part of the landscape but also self-protective: Should I put my raingear on? Do I have enough water for this heat? Dave didn't have raingear or an outer pouch for water bottles—I wasn't sure he had a sweater. There are degrees of letting go. I was susceptible to the elements but he was completely open.

Jumping in with a question I had grappled with for decades, I asked, "Do you think we create our own reality?"

"You mean attracting what we get?"

"Yes."

I thought of Edward, a man I had met at the homeless project where I had volunteered; he had gotten off heroin in jail and was living on the streets. He told of his own monstrous childhood with a pimping, abusive father and addicted mother. When Edward was twelve a policeman took him home and gave him the option to join his family. He stole the officer's gun and robbed a convenience store. How often do we ignore our opportunities?

Then I pictured the argument Hans Jakob and I had had on this same topic. I was taken aback when he so adamantly blamed the victim for poor choices.

I continued, "Like *The Power of Positive Thinking*, *The Secret,* law of attraction, getting the universe to give you what you want, affirmations, storyboards, you know. All of it is repackaged every few years as the newly discovered *power*. How much does God direct what happens to us versus how much do we influence what occurs? Or is it just random?"

Dave asked, "What do you think?" He sounded like he wanted to know.

I loved delving into these topics and it was rare to find someone equally engaged. It was even more rare being asked what I thought. Trying to articulate my ideas, I stammered, "I sense they are all interconnected—somehow—but I can't figure it out." I took a big breath. "To trust the divine means to let go, not sitting on our hands but letting go of results. But to 'ask the universe' implies focusing very hard on a desired goal."

"Are they really so different?"

"What do you mean?"

"We can work with God." Dave went on, "You know that everything is energy."

"The premise of quantum physics." Then I laughed, "I don't really know anything, just what I hear on Science Fridays on the radio."

He laughed with me, a rich belly laugh that filled me with gladness. He said, "Well there are different kinds of energy, like a rock is a lot slower and denser than, say, a thought."

"A thought is energy? Oh, of course, like the power needed to figure out a problem or to express anger," I thought out loud.

"Or to extend love."

"Hmm."

Dave glowed with enthusiasm. "God's resonance is so fine and so fast we can only approximate it with love. Being open and grateful—which is the essence of love—aligns us with heaven."

We walked in silence for a while. The wind tugged at our hats and whipped our pants like sails. *In church we had just prayed "Thy will be done." Lord, help me not to just say the words but to truly attempt to do Your will.*

Dave picked up the thread, "Desiring money, fame, or power comes from lack, which is an offshoot of fear. That is a much lower energy. When we align ourselves with God we are likely to want what we get."

To want what we get rather than get what we want. "I would love to embrace what I get."

* * * *

WE GOT TO TRIACASTELA and Dave waited for me to register at the *albergue*; he was walking on.

"Can I treat you to dinner?"

"That's okay, I'll just keep you company."

I ordered lamb stew and again asked if he would like to share it.

"No, no, I'm fine. Thank you."

The thick fragrant stew came in a good-sized bowl. I set myself the task of finishing it. I was not very hungry; walking distances actually dulled my appetite but I knew I needed to eat because a clothesline was keeping my pants up. When presented with nourishing food, I tried to consume as much as possible.

Dave helped himself to bread and butter, devouring great hunks of the crusty French bread.

The meat was coming-apart tender while the potatoes and carrots remained firm yet soft. The spicy sauce had tomatoes, garlic and onions that left a sharp bite and brought the flavors together.

I was actually done halfway through, but with no way to keep it overnight, I urged myself to eat more. When I couldn't stuff in another bite I pushed the bowl away and—before I could even sigh in satisfaction—Dave grabbed the bowl and gobbled the rest.

To this day I have such piercing regret. Why did I believe his words and not what I saw? Why didn't I risk wasting a few dollars and just order two? I had the opportunity to feed an angel, or saint, or ... who knows? Dave had given me so much nourishment, as much as my cynicism could absorb. I wish so badly I had embraced what I saw in front of me. I wish I had fed him.

"Where are you going after Santiago?" I asked as he picked up his pack.

"I'm walking to Rome … to become a priest."

18—Intentions

WHOA ... I FEEL GOOD ... Like I never thought I would now ...

I belted out my version of the James Brown song and definitely felt good. There was a glimpse of that boundless energy I had when I was young and felt unstoppable.

Onward! Straight through Astorga! Let's shoot for Santa Catalina—that's only six more miles. Yeah, yeah, yeah (I mixed in the Beatles) *... I feel good ...*

Having walked over three hundred miles I was no longer bowed by my backpack and the soles of my feet no longer flinched on cobblestones. Distances that would have sounded impossible a month ago seemed normal and my body accepted, even relished, the daily exertion.

It was a glorious day, perfect light-jacket weather with wispy clouds and a gentle sun. A tractor plowed an open field nearby and sheep grazed unperturbed beside the path. I started humming Bach's *Sheep May Safely Graze* feeling almost safe myself. My faith had grown.

Distrust was still there, mostly in the form of those unfathomable questions: How can You allow all the suffering? Where does pain fit into a divine design? But I began to accept that, like Job, my doubts would never be answered intellectually. Although my conversion from Jew to Catholic had come from academic study, I sensed that trust would not enter through my mind, but only through my heart.

Standing on a bridge, watching the river ripple below, I knew there was no way to will myself to trust; I would have to drop into it, like falling off this bridge. And I felt ready to plunge into that commitment. The possibility of trusting God filled me with well-being and joy. I beamed and opened my arms wide, walking poles dangling from my wrists. Knowing how fleeting this feeling was, I decided to take a picture of the bridge to remind me of the moment.

I pulled out my little digital camera and turned it on. It came alive and the lens started extending—then froze. The whole apparatus was paralyzed; it wouldn't continue, retract, or display anything.

No, no, no. What does this mean? I might need a new camera but—oh, I can't even think of it—have I lost all my precious pictures? It would be like losing the pilgrimage. Lord, what have You done? Here I was learning to trust You and You allow something so dear to me to be destroyed. Okay, I'm being over dramatic. It isn't life threatening—I get that—but this was to be the picture of my step toward trusting You. How about that?

I tried to breathe and regain perspective but my mood had instantly plummeted.

Because the camera was in an awkward half-open position, it could not fit into my pocket or pack. In order to carry it in my hand, I had to strap one pole to my backpack and use the other pole for walking. Then I had to be very careful not to lean too heavily on the one pole because it would stress my shoulder. My I-feel-good walk had turned into a heavy, uneven gait. I pushed on.

Not far from the ill-fated bridge, I noticed a billboard advertising a photography store in the next town, Astorga. Now I had a goal. It seemed surprising that this ad should pop up right when I needed it. I didn't recall seeing any ads for camera stores before—but that synchronistic coincidence failed to penetrate my gloom.

Approaching the outskirts of the city, I was confronted by a towering spiral walkway connected to a bridge leading into town. Not seeing a way around it, I began my labored climb.

Suddenly a tall woman whooshed up, jogging effortlessly around me. Her deft footwork and erect posture beneath a bobbing pack made her look like a poster child for a gym membership.

"Buen Camino," she called speeding ahead.

"Buen, Cam ..." I panted, shaking my head at her prowess. *Jogging, give me a break.*

Even though I had not intended to stay in Astorga, saving my photos overrode any plans to walk farther. As I entered the town I found that the lovely monastery-turned-*albergue* at the entrance only charged 5 Euros so I decided to sign in, reasoning that I could leave my pack while dealing with the camera and, if it took all day, I'd have a place for the night.

The expansive, well-designed hostel housed pilgrims in intimate rooms of four; I was given a slip of paper and tracked down my room and bed assignment. Entering the small dorm I saw, on the bed directly above mine—*oh good grief*—that annoyingly fit jogger. I had been intimidated by her towering strength and now I would be three feet under it.

She was resting on her bunk, lying on her stomach, hugging the pillow.

"Ah, buen Camino again. I'm Sheila," I said flatly.

"Yeh, hello. Meg."

"British?" I guessed.

"Nah, Kiwi."

"That's New Zealand, isn't it?"

"Yeh."

That was enough. I so did not want to do the chitchat. Dumping the pack on my bed I got ready to leave with the camera.

"You travelin' alone?" she asked.

"Yes. Are you?"

"Nah, I'm with meh sis and niece. I jog ahead to get a place and they meet up."

Bully for you. "Well you must be in terrific shape running the Camino." I backed toward the door.

"I keep with it. I'm a copper in a small town."

"A policewoman? That's pretty exciting."

"Yeh, it keeps me goin'. We're not armed. Have to keep fit."

With her bunk at shoulder level, I got a better look. She appeared about forty years old (later I found I was ten years shy), at least six feet tall and powerfully muscular. Short, layered, not quite blond hair framed a no nonsense face with piercing eyes. She had an aura of wary self-sufficiency. I could see how she would be daunting even without a gun.

I had no desire to get to know her and wanted to deal with my own problems as quickly as possible. I turned to leave, yet hesitated. It was baffling—even as it was happening—to find myself moving away from the door and back into the room. There was no conscious decision, no back and forth debate in my mind. Rather I felt tugged—almost unwillingly drawn—to step toward the bunk. In slow motion like a football playback, I inched closer to her. Leaning forward I reached out my arm, slowly extending it up and over the side of the bunk. I placed my hand gently, almost maternally, on her back.

I am not given to approaching strangers and patting them on the back, especially tough looking cops. It felt like an urge to pet a tiger. But I did. I lightly put my hand on her upper back and my fingers imperceptibly stroked her as I would a child.

Then the unimaginable happened. She choked back a sob and, unable to hold it, broke into a flood of tears. I left my hand there as she cried herself out.

"I'm on the Camino for meh daughter," she whispered.

"How nice."

"No, no, no, not nice," she sobbed. "She's dead."

I gasped, "Oh. I'm so—"

"She committed suicide."

Everything stopped in stunned silence. I was frozen by the enormity of her loss. She seemed shocked by her own disclosure.

"Don't tell anyone," she said.

Now we both were crying, our tears mingled on the bare mattress of her bunk.

"I'll pray for her," I murmured.

"I don't believe in that."

"Okay."

We cried for a few more minutes and then stayed together in stillness. The moment eased then dissipated and finally evaporated. We turned away and blew our noses. I sensed she was starting to feel embarrassed and wanted to be left alone, while I felt ashamed at how tragic I had viewed the loss of my camera. I don't remember saying goodbye.

Dazed and drained, I stepped out the door of the *albergue* just as church bells began to ring. I suddenly craved the nourishment of mass. I could see the church one block up and as I crossed the street, a short squat woman joined me.

"*Misa?*" I asked.

"*Ven aqui,*" she responded and grabbed my arm. I was glad to be led.

She proceeded to tow me into the cavernous church and stay by my side, instructing me when to stand and kneel as if I were an unschooled child. It felt strangely comforting to just let her take over. In her grey coat with a white embroidered scarf covering her hair, she looked little but not frail—more like a small boulder.

I knelt, bowing my head: *I'm sorry for my fickleness, Lord. To distrust You because of something as small as photographs. Please bless Meg.*

A faint whisper echoed from the vaulted ceiling: *You bless her.*

What do You mean?

She needs you.

I pushed the thought aside. *Must be a draft in here.*

After mass I showed my Spanish guardian the broken camera; all she said was, "*Ven,*" and again took my arm. We walked together to the photography store but a sign in the window said they were closed for an hour. I never could decipher a pattern for Spanish business hours but my companion seemed completely at ease with it.

"*Té con leche,*" she announced and grabbed me.

Tea sounded great to me. We entered a small café and she ordered biscuits with our drink. I could comprehend a word or two of her blended Spanish-English but she couldn't understand any of mine, so our conversation was limited. What I picked up was that her name was Mary—of course—and that she had always wanted to walk the Camino. With rock-like determination Mary refused to let me pay for our tea. Before we parted, she took my shoulders and turned me toward her, then blessed me with the sign of the cross on my forehead and kissed me on both cheeks. I hugged her then headed back to the store.

"Ah, a leetle jiggling of battery is all it needs," the clerk said. Instantly my camera was set to go. I looked at him in shock. *That's it? Just open the compartment and shake the batteries?* It confirmed my view that technology was an unfathomable mystery. The flip-top cell phone I had left at home occasionally needed its batteries blown on.

The storekeeper also wouldn't let me pay.

But having been properly scared at the prospect of losing my pictures, I asked for all 378 photos to be printed out.

"Ready *una hora*."

"I'll be back," I said and set out to explore.

A flapping red banner caught my eye: Astorga International Chocolate Festival. Entering the large tented arena I found myself among twenty or thirty tables all loaded with mounds of balls, bars, chunks and curlicued chocolate. There were a number of people milling among the displays but the area was so large there was plenty of room to roam. Sloughing off the tensions of the morning I felt giddy with anticipation as I eyed the selections. They were wrapped, plain, nutty, creamed—more possibilities than could be imagined. And every table was giving samples. I ambled about, tasting without restraint. My favorite was the tiny green foil rectangle of Danish milk chocolate that oozed into a puddle in my mouth and simply dissolved.

I am in heaven—the proverbial kid in a candy store.

Most of the Spanish selections were dark, bitter, and strong enough to be rocket fuel, so after sampling my fill I blew out of there on high voltage. I ran to the camera store, picked up my pictures, located the post office, said a quick hello to the pilgrims sending their superfluous gear home, packaged my photographs and sent them off, then flew out.

Outside the post office, directly in front of me, was a fancy looking hotel advertising massages. Throwing financial caution to the wind I entered the marble and glass lobby and plunked down 40 Euros. I was led into a studio where I luxuriated in a long hot shower then laid down on the massage table. My speediness stilled and I sank into a floating sensation, drifting toward sleep. The aroma of lavender and musk swirled around me as lotion seeped into my back and coaxed my muscles out of their knots. Peeking from half closed eyes I saw that my masseuse was a lovely black-haired, chocolate-colored woman with catlike movements. She told me her name was Adilah, that she had moved to Spain from Morocco and missed her family terribly. The scent of the oil, the Spanish-Arabic music, her soothing touch and quiet voice, lulled me to minimal consciousness. When she finished I didn't move. Adilah left and a few minutes later returned with a slip of paper.

"Here are the names of my family." She hesitated, seemingly shy to ask, "Will you carry them to Santiago?"

"I'd be honored to."

Looking at the floor, she whispered, "And have them blessed at the cathedral?"

"Of course."

I got up and tucked the paper into my waist pack with my money and passport. I shook my head at this day of unexpected connections. In addition to Adilah and her family I would carry Meg and her deceased daughter with me to be blessed in Santiago—even if she didn't believe in it.

Floating out of the hotel, I decided I needed more sustenance than biscuits and chocolate so I wandered into a nearby café, sat at the bar, and ordered the paella. When I was told it would take an hour I didn't mind just staying perched on the stool doing nothing. As I sipped my wine I kept thinking back to Meg. *Did that encounter really happen? Was she okay the rest of the day?*

The cook brought my dish and an aroma of garlic and tomato wafted up from the platter of reddish rice, sausage, chicken, and whole shrimp with their eyes bulging up at me. The round, grey-haired cook in a flowered apron said she had once served this dish to Frank Sinatra and pointed to a glossy picture of him with his arm around her. While she recounted her other famous patrons, *My Way* and *It Was a Very Good Year* flitted through my mind. I ate everything except the shrimp, leaving a pile of eyes and antennae in the middle of the plate.

"*Muchas gracias.*" I pushed my plate away.

Full beyond replete, I was drawn from the café to the center square by American-sounding shouts and cheers. Ten lanky teens had worked up an acrobatic and juggling demonstration—balancing on each other's shoulders and throwing balls about. The tricks were simple but performed with contagious enthusiasm as they yelled encouragement to each other: "Good job!" "Way to go!" Their teacher, a short, trim cleric in a Roman collar, stood smiling nearby.

"Are you from the States?" I asked the priest. "And hiking the Camino?"

He turned his smile to me. "We're from St. Alban's, a small Catholic high school in Pennsylvania. We're walking the Camino with no money, relying on the donations we get from the shows."

"Wow! How do you know you'll have enough?"

"We believe God will provide."

"Has He?"

"More or less, but always enough."

"That is amazing faith." I stuffed a handful of Euros in their bag.

As I headed back toward the *albergue* my steps slowed to a crawl. My head drooped in embarrassment. *Those kids trust You with their lives while I abandoned You because of a camera.* I sighed, still looking down. *I'm sorry. My focus was so set. I wanted to walk straight through this town and hated having my plans thwarted. Was it Your intention I come here?*

Entering the dorm room, I met Meg's sister, Joan, and niece, Catherine. Meg and I looked at each other and silently nodded. I recognized the powerful jock but now could see her underlying frailty; I was curious what she saw beneath my veneer. Immediately Joan and Catherine filled up the space with chatter. "Oh we found the most wonderful chocolate at this festival. We bought several bars." They pulled out four large rectangles of Belgian chocolate and—just for that day— my stomach recoiled at the sight of more chocolate.

They continued, "We picked up these shirts in town. Aren't they adorable?" They were showing me their loot and I wondered who was going to lug all that. I was sure they knew about Meg's daughter, but didn't think they were aware how much sorrow she carried.

"Looks like you had a good day," I said.

"Oh it was lovely," Joan answered, "but we're bloody tire' from all the walkin'." She glanced at me as she rewrapped all her goodies. "You?"

"It was ..." A swirl of garlic, chocolate, and lavender lotion, tea, mass and blessings, photos and boys springing off their partners' shoulders swept through my mind. I looked at Meg, remembering our tears blended together on her mattress. "It was amazing."

"We really ought to exchange emails just'n case we're ever in the States, don't you think?'

"Sure," I said though I thought the chance of our getting together was about as great as spotting flying pigs. I did not give out my email casually, but in this case I figured it would evaporate in the enormous distance between us.

Meg said quietly, "I ... I'd ... like that."

So we exchanged information and the next morning said our hurried goodbyes. I was sure that was the end of it. In addition to living on opposite sides of the world, Meg and I had nothing in common. What could an almost seventy-year-old, American, Catholic, retired dance teacher, and a fifty-year-old, nonreligious, New Zealand policewoman have to say to one another?

* * * *

YET WHEN I GOT HOME we began writing sporadic emails. Meg talked about her deceased daughter and her ex-husband; she described just-for-fun weekly runs up a mountain; her move from corporate to cop and future dreams of becoming a personal trainer and massage therapist. She mentioned that her sister, Joan, had been diagnosed with breast cancer and that she was helping her with the chemo treatments. It became clear that Meg's tough exterior was a gossamer veil over a beautifully tender heart.

I told her of my empty nest and how difficult it was to inch fully into retirement. I opened up to her how I hated aging, how it was a daily battle to keep any positive outlook for the future.

About a year later, Meg wrote, "I met someone special." I could almost see her blush through the computer. She continued, "He used to work in the States."

"How about a visit then?" I offered.

"I've never been there."

"We'll plan on it. You'll stay here."

We ironed out the details and, soon after, they bought tickets.

Then it turned out that the day Meg and Teddy were due to arrive I had to be at a family reunion, so I arranged for a friend to pick them up, introduce them to my house and car, and hand over the keys. The doors of my life were flung open to a woman I had met for less than an hour and her boyfriend who I had never seen.

"Egad," my friend moaned, "do you normally offer your car and house to people you meet on the street?"

"Uh ... not often."

As it turned out, Meg and Teddy entered my life and filled it to the brim. We talked, laughed, drank, toured, and ate our way through their visit. At the end of their three-week stay, when normally I would have been relieved to wave goodbye to houseguests, I already missed them.

"Nex' year yeh come to us, ay?" Meg invited.

I breathed in the growing love between us. Having walked the Camino alone, I had returned with an entire family.

(My New Zealand friend approved this chapter for publication. It is dedicated to her deceased daughter.)

19—Fifth Extraordinary Encounter: Carrying The Cross

AFTER REACHING SANTIAGO, a lot of pilgrims pushed on, trekking an additional sixty miles to Finisterre, the "end of the world." But I was done. I was proud of having walked every step of the five hundred miles from Roncesvalles to Santiago and had no need to go after a Super Pilgrim badge. Yet I couldn't go home without seeing the most western tip of Europe. The outcropping had been considered sacred since Druid times and legends held that St. James had visited, died, and been buried there for a while. That speck of land beckoned me. What would I find at the end of the world?

I was striding across Santiago toward the bus station when I bumped into a woman I had briefly met before. She spoke a fast, flowing French; from what I could understand, she had just gotten back from Finisterre and highly recommended the little pension where she had stayed. Even though I was anxious to get going, she insisted on drawing a map of how to find it. Thanking her, I mindlessly tucked it in my pocket and hurried off.

When I saw the bus going to Finisterre, it looked like an ordinary, large, long-distance vehicle. The first clue that this would not be a typical Greyhound ride was that the luggage holds were simply open for passengers to dump their belongings in whatever manner they chose. The bus stopped at numerous towns along the way and, because the luggage was stored so haphazardly, every stop required all of it to be removed and reshuffled so the departing passengers could get their bags. Then we had to wait as the driver took the new customer's money, made change, and chatted with them.

Even though the bus looked modern and well equipped there was no bathroom on it. At one point the driver pulled over to the side of a highway; a man jumped off and ran to the middle of an open field, turned his back to us, and peed for a very long time. The entire busload of passengers clapped and cheered at his return. I prayed I would never need the same service.

The ride took five and a half hours for a three-hour trip. At first I was riddled with frustration at the inefficient waste of time. By the end it didn't matter. I had become encased in the *Camino Tranquilo*, the sense that everything was progressing at the appropriate speed.

Getting off the bus, I noticed that the municipal *albergue* was nearby in the center of town. Had I not had that map, along with the French woman's enthusiastic recommendation, I would simply have signed in there. Somehow the map was a pull—like other tugs on the Camino—to the hilltop refuge of Casa Velay. I climbed the hill, stopping several times to catch my breath and shake my head: Why was I following these scribbled directions from a near stranger?

I registered and clambered up the steep stairs to my room. Glancing at the lovely brass double bed with a fluffy white comforter, I went straight to the open window facing the ocean. My room hung over a small cove with sparkling sand. The sun played with the clouds forming patterns of light and shadow and, among them, I noticed what looked like a crucifix planted at the edge of the beach. The small statue sat on top of a tall pole like a mast on a ship. Salty sea air gently blew my hair and filled me with what felt like the most delicious food.

Realizing I hadn't eaten all day I scurried out, found a grocery store near the beach and bought bread, cheese, tomatoes, and olives. I sat on the ridge overlooking the ocean and used a plastic knife to make a sandwich. Suddenly the wind picked up. It turned violent, swirling around me, rolling olives and flapping the paper about. I quickly scrunched everything together and scooted down the steps of the cove for shelter. Relieved that the bottom step was protected, I put the sandwich back together and happily tore off big hunks speckled with sand. The juicy tomato, spicy olives, and crusty French bread perfectly complemented the tangy Machego cheese. I felt utterly content sitting in my little nest, munching and looking around.

Crucifixes are scattered throughout the Spanish countryside so I had not paid any attention to the one at the beach. Now, sitting on the step gave me a different view: I noticed it had two figures.

Inching closer I peered at the images carved in weathered grey stone. The wind died down and I walked around it as I licked my fingers from the last of that hefty sandwich. On one side of the carving was a standard crucifix, the Lord hanging from the cross, beams large enough to be seen above and beside Him. On the opposite side, like the other face of a coin, St. James seemed to hang from the same cross. I had never seen a crucifix like this and briefly puzzled over what it meant. But I pushed the thoughts away, trying to distance myself from the usual discomfort I felt with Christ's gruesome passion.

Bone weariness fell over me. Grabbing my things, I pulled myself together enough to climb up to my room and throw myself on the inviting bed. The gentle lap of the ocean and the cool salted breeze expanded my lungs and lulled me into a dreamless sleep. An hour later I woke up refreshed and energized.

I packed a little bag with water and camera, grabbed my poles, and headed out on the three-mile walk to the official tip of the continent. The steep road was dotted with hiking pilgrims as well as tourists in cars and buses on their way to this famous site. Reaching the rocky promontory, I marveled at the beauty of the coast and at the number of boots, headbands, rosaries, and written requests that had been left on a concrete cross near the edge. This was the end point of many journeys.

Beautiful as it was, my mind kept going back to the crucifix in the cove near my room. I don't know why I wanted to see it again. Glancing around one last time, I took my leave of the world's end.

As I hiked down I was delighted to see Nicolas walking up—Nico was the León angel who had gotten me garlic soup. When we had first met, he had told me about coming on the Camino to be with his girlfriend; he had proposed but she had refused and left him on the trail.

We flew into a hug.

"Are you still searching for soup?" he teased.

"No," I laughed. "I feel fine."

He invited me to join his group for a sundowner party, but I declined and asked, "Nico, did you get what you wanted from the walk?"

He touched my shoulder like a blessing. "I am at peace."

I gave him another hug then scooted down the hill, straight to the double image crucifix. I walked round and round the statue. As I looked more closely, it appeared that Jesus not only hung on but also hoisted the cross with St. James on it. Likewise, St. James seemed to carry the cross with Christ on it. The ancient craftsman had managed to make each figure appear to lift the other.

Hmmm, I reflected, *the Lord carries us—okay I get that— but are we then to help Him by shouldering His pain?* St. James followed Jesus into martyrdom, being beheaded by Herod in 42 A.D. I am not a big fan of martyrdom and that seemed an unfathomable cross to bear.

Lord, Your passion scares me. I have never understood it and don't really want to face it. Why did You have to bear such torture? We are so often told that Your agony has saved us from our sins. How could that possibly be? And why do some people have to endure so much more than others? What good is all this suffering anyway?

It was an age-old, often-asked lament, more of a wail than real questions. I wasn't seeking, certainly not expecting, an answer. So it was a tingling, goose-bump surprise to hear the wind and waves whisper a response:

If there were no suffering you would be like the grass.

Grass?

Uh-huh.

Not even an animal?

Completely unconscious.

I had to think about that. Suffering creates consciousness? Without travail we'd sink past the animal kingdom to simple fodder? I pictured some of the private school children I worked with, kids who had all the bumps in their world leveled, and how they seemed to be sound asleep in their own entitlement. I thought back to the Gurdjieff teachings I had studied, where he emphasized the need for friction to make us more aware. If everything went our way we would never have to question who we are and where God is.

But I didn't like it. It was painful to accept Christ as victim, and to consider what that meant for us. I saw it as another form of that notion—the difficult to accept and even harder to hold onto realization—that we need to be grateful for what grows us. St. Ignatius said it clearly when he directed us to welcome *whatever* gets us closer to God.

Part of me wanted to crawl back to my cozy bed and hide from this encounter, while another part wanted to just stay with the crucifix. I went to my little step and sat down. My brain spun like that multi-colored, overload wheel on the computer. I couldn't grasp anything and didn't want to try. Like on the bus coming in, it occurred to me to let go, to just release all the questions and the striving to understand.

Throughout the journey, the Spanish sky had consistently appeared more vivid than any I had seen in California and now the royal blue above me deepened. A shower of gold exploded from between the clouds. Dazzling yellows and rich oranges streaked across the horizon, making everything glow. I watched the golden tones brighten into vibrant pinks and blazing reds illuminating the entire sky, setting the heavens on fire. Then after a while—I had no idea how long I sat gaping—the colors softened and diminished into shades of violet. And they faded away.

There were no words and no thoughts. I melted into mindless awe.

I had the sense that this was my last extraordinary encounter and the spectacular lightshow was my grand finale. I felt open and at peace. I would not leave boots or a bandana here, but for just this evening I could leave my struggle.

The *Camino Tranquilo* urged me to rest on the irrational belief that all was well, everything was proceeding as it was meant to be.

Epilogue: Pulling the Thread

EARLY ONE MORNING a mutual friend called to tell me Reed had been taken to the hospital. I was taken aback by the news but not surprised. In the three years after walking the Camino, Reed and I had spent more time together but there was less hiking and more helping. The latest cancer surgery had not worked and he was clearly in decline—even sharing trail stories had become too much for him.

The call came when I was in the middle of packing for a month-long, wide-ranging trip to the other side of the world. Ever since Meg and Teddy had visited last year, the idea of going Down Under had taken hold. And this forthcoming journey was a Camino-like leap into the unknown, a let's-see-what-happens kind of adventure.

I stopped mid-fold and rushed out.

At this hour there was little traffic and I flew into the emergency department. Reed was lying still with his eyes closed. He looked like a cadaver and emanated a sodden flower scent, which, mixed with the hospital antiseptic, made me feel queasy. The one chair in the cubicle was wedged right next to his bed, but there was nowhere else to sit so I perched on the edge of the seat and tried to breathe without inhaling too much.

In a few minutes he opened his eyes. They were round and frightened like a dog caught in a trap.

"Thank you for coming." His voice sounded hoarse but not as weak as I expected.

"You couldn't keep me away," I said, knowing I would have given anything to be anywhere else.

Silence. Was it the lack of conversation that had always plagued us or was it that, at this point, there was not much to say?

"Can I get you anything?" I retreated to my go-to care-taking role.

"Well ..." He seemed hesitant to ask. "Do you have a nail file? I hate seeing my nails so long."

Rummaging in my pack-like bag, I found a half-used emery board. I was relieved to have a task but his skin and nails were so yellow I was reluctant to touch him. Scolding myself for being unkind, I gently took his cold dry hand and started filing.

"Thank you."

I needed clippers and a proper metal nail file to accomplish anything; this felt like trying to smooth a log with a piece of waxed paper. But it gave us something to do and the slight rasping sound filled the silence.

"My brother's coming in," Reed said.

"That's good."

"No. He takes over everything. But I am not going to let him take this over."

Reed had battled his rare form of stomach cancer for years. I had not known when I first met him, when he had introduced me to the whole idea of walking the Camino, that he had already undergone the first of three operations trying to stem the tide of this relentless disease.

Scrape, scrape ... the nail of his right forefinger started to curve as I leaned into my task.

A doctor came in. Squat frame with a shock of black hair, starched white coat and rumpled eyes, he pulled a chair from another room and sat down. The space was so cramped his knee grazed mine.

"I'm Dr. Yonemura. I admitted you last night." He dove right in speaking deliberately. "This is how it is. We can unhook you from the hydration and feeding machines and you'll be dead in a week." Surprisingly it sounded factual rather than harsh, like a weather report.

I was startled into a slight sweat suddenly finding myself completely present and not a smidge elsewhere.

"No." Reed's voice was also even. "I'm not ready to die yet. Send me home with all the tubes."

"Okay.

Hospice accepted the case and within hours Reed was brought home and set up in a hospital bed in his living room. I was leaving for New Zealand the next day.

"Are you ready to go?" he asked me between morphine-induced naps.

"Yes, mostly packed." I felt guilty having my travel adventures ahead of me when Reed would have loved to just be able to walk to the bathroom.

"I'm getting ready too."

My throat constricted with unshed tears. He was facing the ultimate journey. As much as any of us is connected, that last mile is completely alone.

I told him I loved him and he said he loved me too. Why had we never spoken those words before?

"Buen Camino," I said.

"Buen Camino." He raised his hand as if to wave. The nail on his right forefinger looked round and pretty.

* * * *

I WALKED HOME from Reed's house with my head bowed. As I returned to packing it occurred to me that I was going Down Under while he was headed Up Above. Reed would have loved the image. I had argued that the trip could be postponed but he insisted I not change my travel plans; I had bookings in New Zealand, Tasmania, Australia, and Malaysia. He enjoyed hearing the extravagant arrangements of this new pilgrimage, said my trip sounded daring. I knew his journey required raw courage.

For this Camino I was taking a battered carry-on suitcase rather than a backpack and my disassembled walking poles were wedged inside it. The poles were sheathed in ordinary rubber tips rather than the crazy champagne corks Reed had made. I loved his corks but they didn't actually work to grip the trail so I had safely stored them in my dresser drawer. The pilgrim's clamshell he had given me would have been destroyed banging on a suitcase, so I put it away too.

As I laid out my boots and light jacket, I smiled seeing the exact clothes I had worn to Spain a few years ago. Rather than follow the tradition of burning one's pilgrim clothes, I liked the idea of wearing them on a new expedition. Glancing at my watch—identical to the one that broke on the Camino—I saw I had less than twenty-four hours before departure. My heart started its wacky thumping. Time to check-in online.

* * * *

"LADIES AND GENTS, twenty minutes to touch down at Auckl'in."

The announcement startled me awake. My gum was wedged in the side of my mouth and I was drooling. *Good heavens, I had thirteen hours to snooze and my ornery body chooses right before landing to fall into a dead sleep.* Disoriented and grumpy, I fumbled about preparing to disembark.

My lanky New Zealand seatmates had slept for most of the flight and were frowzily pulling themselves together for landing. They stretched and rummaged the bins for their belongings. Meanwhile I began to fidget, dabbing at the faint stain on my shirt left from a mystery-meat pie, then pulling out my itinerary.

Reed would not have chosen this trip; he wanted to walk the Camino Frances again. I had no desire to return to the Santiago pilgrimage because I was afraid my expectations would influence what I saw: This is where I met so-and-so and here is where that vision happened. I did not think I could see the trail with fresh eyes and was happy to leave the Camino to a special, sacred memory. Now I was on the way to form new memories.

I looked at my current travel plans. The thick wad of papers was already dog-eared from being studied over and over. The top sheet was my ticket to Auckland where I would be staying with Meg. Our brief meeting on the Camino had blossomed into a bond encircling the world and I was now enmeshed in the lives of Meg, her sister, her boyfriend and his children. We were even talking about Teddy's son living with me if he decided to go to university in the States.

I had begun my five-hundred-mile walk alone and reached the end in a crowd. It was like that saying when a butterfly flaps its wings in China an earthquake hits California, or something like that. I did not know my flapping wings would unite me with so many people and, dissimilar as we were, how strong the connections would become.

My reason for going Down Under was to visit Meg but I wanted to take advantage of traveling this far, so the second sheet confirmed my stay at the Pickled Frog hostel in Hobart, Tasmania, and with it a hike down Mt. Wellington. Then it was off to Katoomba, Australia, where I had booked a walkabout in the Australian bush with an aboriginal guide. Inserted between those two pages was my travel insurance receipt assuring me I could be medivaced out of anywhere.

I still thought of myself as timid and it was hard to believe I was taking this adventurous trip. I hadn't thought the Camino had changed me that much. Sure I had come back a bit thinner and calmer but both my weight and tranquility had crept back to normal. Yet ... I saw myself knock down a pesky wasp nest from the overhang of my house, sign up for an advanced dance class when I usually took intermediate, and tell that ungenerous fellow I was seeing that it was not working out. And plan this trip.

"Last check for tray tables and chair backs, folks."

Flight attendants strode down the aisles making sure we were ready for our final descent. As anxious as I was to get off the plane I was terrified to venture out. I peeked at the last page while folding my itinerary back into my pants pocket. I was ending in Kuala Lumpur to meet my friend, Sister Pat, and spend five days in a Malaysian convent. Living as a nun was what I was looking forward to the most and that desire showed me how the Camino had truly changed me.

My cynical, skeptical nature had evolved. On the trail I was consistently startled when something worked out—every available bed, every saved fall, every new friend, every offered kindness took me completely by surprise. I never anticipated a good result and was astonished when one happened. Now I was more open and welcoming to the divine in my life. The *I-Will-Never-Get-A-Bed* fear inched closer to *Things-Might-Work-Out* optimism—and I was quicker to say "Thank You" when they did. Striving to walk with God began to include the possibility that He might want to walk with me.

The plane jolted into touchdown and I pulled out my phone. Switching from airplane mode, I scrolled through a slew of emails and ads then felt an internal jolt. There was a message from Reed's brother: Memorial service for Reed. My feelings swooped and swirled. The sorrow of losing him intertwined with relief that he was out of pain. Above all I felt grateful for Reed in my life. If it weren't for Reed I would never have walked the Camino: I would not have met angels, picked up a sandal, danced with a nun, or melted into a massage. Because of Reed I have wept in gratitude at extraordinary visions of God's love. And because of him I was walking out the door of the Auckland airport toward a new pilgrimage. Taking a deep breath of the pre-dawn morning air, I pictured both of us starting our journeys at the same time.

* * * *

MIDNIGHT IN A narrow, open cavern in New Zealand, Meg and I lean back in our kayak with our heads tilted up. I sigh in amazement to be so far from home and with a woman who is now a dear friend. Three years ago, almost to the month, we brushed past each other on the Camino, like I had with so many others throughout that journey. Who could have predicted that our connection would grow and encompass so much of our lives?

The water gently laps against the sides of our kayak as we look about. The cavern is just a few feet wide allowing us to see only a slice of sky between the towering rock walls. We glimpse the shimmering stars, clear and bright against their black background. Then I notice that the sides of the cave are also lit up—Meg smiles as she watches me take in the unlikely sparkle alongside us.

"What's that?" I ask astonished.

"Poop."

"What?"

"It's the remains of glowworm poop." Meg delights in my puzzlement.

Both of us stare in awe at the rock sides; back and forth we study the sky and the sides. We gasp as it dawns on us that the glowing sides of the cavern perfectly match the sky above. The celestial lights and the glowworm poop form what looks like identical patterns.

Meg had been here before but had not focused on the luminous replication. "How can the heavens above and the dung below look so much the same?" Meg asks. "How could this be chance?" A stunning question from a woman who disdains religion.

Dazzled by the universe-sized possibilities, I murmur, "I hope ... I feel like it's intentional."

"You mean planned?"

"Well, who knows if the stars and the poop are precisely identical—they look like it but ..." I rub my neck, which is getting sore from looking up. "More importantly they remind me of the many times I've felt a divine hand in this world—'on earth as it is in heaven.'"

My mind goes back to Spain and all the "coincidences" that led me to connect with Meg: my broken camera outside of Astorga, the annoying meeting with her on the overpass, the chance location of our beds in such a large hostel. Most of all I marvel at the unconscious pull I had felt to put my hand on her back. That simple gesture was astounding—even to me—because it was so unlikely. Where had the impulse come from?

Looking at the sparkling lights around us, I breathe in the present. I feel so *here*, so linked to the stars, my friend, the kayak, the poop. I sense the infinite within this one moment and a fluttering joy expands my heart. "I think meeting you ... and going on the Camino ... and all the journeys taken and yet to come are intended," I say. "I believe it."

About the Author

Sheila Kogan has been a dance teacher most of her life. She has written a teacher's guide, *Step by Step: A Complete Movement Education Curriculum* and a children's book, *Lambs of Fairy Glen: An Almost True Story*. Visit her at sheilakogan.com

Honest, inspiring, funny and humble, Sheila guides us along the Camino and her deeply personal pilgrimage. *Found Along The Way* is for anyone contemplating a spiritual journey, regardless of faith. Reading this book, you might not walk the Camino yourself, but you will make friends with someone who has.

Alon Shalev, author of the award-winning Wycaan Master series.

Whimsical yet cuts to the bone, *Found Along The Way* takes the reader on an adventure, making unexpected friendships and invigorating one's soul. Uplifting.

Barbara Hawkins *Writer/Virtual Traveler,* author of *Behind the Forgotten Front*

Having never walked the Camino de Santiago, I now know what I might encounter having read Sheila Kogan's *Found Along The Way*. What I found was disarming honesty and fresh images, story after story. She writes of encounters, both with God and total strangers who became friends—even angels when such were needed.

Reverend Thomas P. Sweetser, SJ, director of the Parish Evaluation Project, author of *Can Francis Change the Church?*

Her discoveries on The Camino are reminders of the grace and majesty of living.

Tim Campbell, PhD, World Bank Specialist for twenty years, author of *Beyond Smart Cities*, and *The Quiet Revolution*

This delightful book is much more than memories of the Camino, it is a journey of a walk with God told in a very courageous and honest way. Her Extraordinary Encounters follow the example of Jesus by using everyday images to show a deep truth.

Sister Lorna Walsh. SSHJM. BSc. Dip Th.
Chigwell Convent, Essex, UK